Games, Ideas and Activities for Primary PSHE

Games, Ideas and Activities for Primary PSHE

Julie McCormick and Robin Whyler

PEARSON

Harlow, England • London • New York • Boston • San Francisco • Toronto • Sydney
Auckland • Singapore • Hong Kong • Tokyo • Seoul • Taipei • New Delhi
Cape Town • São Paulo • Mexico City • Madrid • Amsterdam • Munich • Paris • Milan

PEARSON EDUCATION LIMITED
Edinburgh Gate
Harlow CM20 2JE
United Kingdom
Tel: +44 (0)1279 623623
Fax: +44 (0)1279 431059
Website: www.pearson.com/uk

First edition published in Great Britain in 2012

© Julie McCormick and Robin Whyler 2012

The rights of Julie McCormick and Robin Whyler to be identified as authors of this work
have been asserted by them in accordance with the Copyright, Designs and Patents Act 1988.

Pearson Education is not responsible for the content of third-party internet sites.

ISBN: 978-1-4082-6774-5

British Library Cataloguing in Publication Data
A CIP catalogue record for this book can be obtained from the British Library

Library of Congress Cataloging in Publication Data
McCormick, Julie.
  Games, ideas, and activities for primary PSHE / Julie McCormick and Robin Whyler.
    p. cm.
  ISBN 978-1-4082-6774-5 (limp)
  1. Social skills--Study and teaching (Elementary)--Activity programs. 2. Health education (Elementary)
I. Whyler, Robin. II. Title.
  LB1139.S6.M33 2012
  302.14071--dc23
                              2011051074

10 9 8 7 6 5 4 3 2 1
16 15 14 13 12

Set by 30
Printed and bound in Malaysia (CTP-VP)

Contents

Introduction

Personal, Social and Health Education (PSHE) is a subject that is taught from Reception to Year 11. It is a subject that is open to different interpretations and our book is designed to complement the curriculum in KS1 and KS2.

PSHE contributes to the personal and social skills needed for children's futures. It gives children the confidence to deal with everyday situations. The children gain knowledge and independence in how to ask for information and where to go to get help. PSHE also gives them the skills to take greater responsibility to become more active members of their community and of the wider society. PSHE teaches children the rules of society, both social and moral. By introducing them to all the concepts of PSHE it helps them to appreciate what it means to be a positive member of a diverse and multi-cultural society.

PSHE is a subject that cannot be delivered in isolation from the other areas of the curriculum. We think that PSHE is equally important and is there to help to build upon all areas of the curriculum. In the activities covered we have tried to emphasise the importance of including children in asking questions, participating in problem-solving activities and exploring issues.

In a number of the ideas we have suggested asking members of the community to come in and speak about their experiences. It is important that the ideas and concepts of PSHE are, wherever possible, reinforced with real world examples, allowing children to meet positive and supportive role models. Children should be encouraged to think about others and to empathise with different situations. We are giving the children the opportunities to take action, to be positive and to feel in control in all different kinds of circumstances.

Analogies are also a good way to teach areas of PSHE as they require 'jumps' of understanding that are memorable and empowering. Care should be taken to judge the class and make sure it is not a leap too far! Role-play is also a good tool in teaching PSHE. It allows children to think about the situations that are specific to them and to those around them as well as learning and practising key skills to deal with life's situations.

When writing the book we have been aware that some of the areas of the curriculum are complex and the teacher could feel overwhelmed as to how to get the objectives across. We have therefore tried to make these activities as clear and enjoyable as possible. These activities should be delivered through a balance of adult and child led participation, allowing children to explore the topics, make mistakes and feel central to the lesson. Above all, the manner in which the lesson is taught is as important as the lesson itself.

Asking children's personal opinions and understanding of the topics should be the starting point to make the lessons as relevant and central to their own lives as possible. One of the most important skills that PSHE should teach children is the ability to think for themselves, to analyse situations based on a greater knowledge and experience base, allowing them to make decisions that are right for them.

The overall objectives can be roughly summed up as follows:

- To know and understand what is meant by a healthy lifestyle
- To be aware of safety issues
- To understand what makes good relationships with others
- To have respect for others
- To be thoughtful and responsible members of their community and their school
- To become active members of our democratic society
- To develop self-confidence and self-esteem
- To make informed choices regarding personal and social issues
- To develop good relationships with other members of the community.

We have tried to keep the book's layout as simple and clear as possible, devoting a chapter to each of the four main areas that the curriculum covers:

- Developing confidence and responsibility and making the most of their abilities
- Preparing to play an active role as citizens
- Developing a healthy, safer lifestyle
- Developing good relationships and respecting the differences between people.

In each of these chapters we have divided the ideas into KS1 and KS2 (although many can be adapted for use across both). Each idea is accompanied by details of exactly which part of the curriculum it has been written for and the ideas are listed in the same order as the objectives.

Wherever possible we have put cross-curriculum links and wherever helpful a basic worksheet that can be used as is or adapted to suit.

Some of the core ideas will be recognisable to more experienced teachers. The same good ideas tend to be used and passed around the length and breadth of the country, almost like folklore! They vary through constant adaption, resurfacing time and again.

We hope this book will take a lot of the stress out of research and will act as a good source or foundation for your own personalised PSHE lesson plans, giving you a few more precious moments in the evening to recharge your batteries!

Chapter 1

Developing confidence and responsibility and making the most of their abilities

Introduction

Some of the following activities can be used for KS1 and KS2 but it is really for the teacher to use their discretion knowing the ability of their class.

There are eleven areas that need to be covered in KS1 and KS2 in this chapter. All the activities have been laid out following this order and below each title is a full description of which one it relates to.

Key Stage 1

In Key Stage 1 the children are encouraged to begin to learn about themselves by becoming aware of different feelings and opinions as well as beginning to explore their own strengths that can build self-esteem. There are five main areas that need to be covered in Key Stage 1:

- To recognise what they like and dislike, what is fair and unfair, and what is right and wrong
- To share their opinions on things that matter to them and explain their views
- To recognise, name and deal with their feelings in a positive way
- To think about themselves, learn from their experiences and recognise what they are good at
- To know how to set simple goals.

Key Stage 2

As well as developing key ways to continue to build self-esteem and face daily challenges with a balanced outlook, Key Stage 2 introduces themes that will become increasingly important as the children get older. These include money, emotions, communication and an awareness of how their skills could potentially be used in choosing what they may want to do in the future. Here are the six areas that need to be covered:

- To talk and write about their opinions and explain their views on issues that affect themselves and society
- To recognise their worth as individuals by identifying positive things about themselves and their achievements, seeing their mistakes, making amends and setting personal goals
- To face new challenges positively by collecting information, looking for help, making responsible choices and taking action

- To recognise, as they approach puberty, how people's emotions change at that time and how to deal with their feelings towards themselves, their family and others in a positive way
- To learn about the range of jobs carried out by people they know and to understand how they can develop skills to make their own contribution in the future
- To look after their money and realise that future wants and needs may be met through saving.

KS1

Ideas

I know!

To be able, with simple statements, to get children to question the reasons why they feel a certain way.

Suitable for and curriculum fulfilment

- KS1
- Developing confidence and responsibility and making the most of their abilities
- To recognise what they like and dislike, what is fair and unfair, and what is right and wrong

Aims

- To begin to get children to explore their own feelings and their understanding of fairness
- To feel comfortable discussing these feelings in a group

Resources

- Small whiteboard and a whiteboard marker

What to do

- In circle time ask the children to think about what they like or dislike, what they find fair or unfair, and what is right and wrong.
- Explain that you are going to write statements that they are to finish, thinking about how they feel.
- Write a sentence on the whiteboard, e.g. I feel angry when ... (child to complete).
- Ask another child to read the sentence and the class to discuss and make suggestions.
- React to their answers and find out if feeling angry is because something is unfair, wrong or is it unjustified.
- Write another sentence on the whiteboard, e.g. When it is sunny I feel ... (child to complete).

- Ask the next child to read the sentence and the class to discuss and make suggestions.
- A possible response may be – When it is sunny I feel happy. The teacher can ask why it makes them feel happy. Is feeling happy something we like?
- Continue using some of these statements:
  When it is snowing I feel ... When it is raining I feel ... When I don't listen I feel ... When someone isn't my friend I feel ... A bully can make me feel ... A friend can make me feel ...

Variations/extensions

- Statements can be made into cards and laminated; each child can choose a card

Cross-curriculum link

- Literacy

What I like

It is important for children to recognise what they like and dislike and that others can like and dislike different things. They should be able to think about why they like and dislike things and feel comfortable telling others.

Suitable for and curriculum fulfilment

- KS1
- Developing confidence and responsibility and making the most of their abilities
- To recognise what they like and dislike, what is fair and unfair, and what is right and wrong

Aims

- To get children to understand that they have a right to an opinion and learn how to explore and express the reasons why they hold this opinion
- To understand that we can all like different things

Resources

- Images of different foods
- Whiteboard and digital projector (optional)
- Worksheet with 'Foods I like' written at the top and a box for a picture with caption space below

What to do

- Show the class all kinds of different images of food and ask them to name them all.
- Ask the children to draw their favourite food on the worksheet, writing the name of the food and why they like it.
- They can also draw a simple face with an expression of how the food makes them feel.

- Ask individual children to show their worksheet and tell the class what they like and why.
- Applaud them when they finish.
- Discuss with the class that we all like different things.
- Display the worksheets on the wall for a couple of days where children will see them.

Variations/extensions

- A variety of subjects can be used, e.g. what I like to do at the weekend, what games I like to play, my favourite toy

Cross-curriculum link

- Science

Bespoke resource

- See worksheet in Bespoke resources chapter at the end of the book

My weekend

This is a good activity to do on a Monday morning. In circle time, every child shares with the class the highs and lows of their weekend.

Suitable for and curriculum fulfilment

- KS1
- Developing confidence and responsibility and making the most of their abilities
- To share their opinions on things that matter to them and explain their views

Aim

- To get children to share their views on things that matter to them

Resources

- None needed

What to do

- Set out some simple rules for sharing their 'Weekend News', e.g. listen to your friends and sit still.
- In turn ask the children their weekend news.
- Encourage the class to ask two or three questions, e.g. 'I went to the park this weekend ...'
  - Did you have a nice time?
  - Did you see any other friends there?
  - What did you do in the park?
- Encourage the children to express their feelings about what they did or what happened.
- Help the children to explain their views clearly with helpful questions.

Variations/extensions

- Have the class keep a Monday diary and write about their weekend news

Cross-curriculum link

- Literacy

Our school environment

This activity is to get the children to see their immediate surroundings from an environmental point of view (water, electricity, heat, recycling and paper use) and how they are responsible and interconnected to their environment. This will also help develop their confidence in talking about and sharing each other's opinions and views.

Suitable for and curriculum fulfilment

- KS1
- Developing confidence and responsibility and making the most of their abilities
- To share their opinions on things that matter to them and explain their views

Aims

- To get the children to be aware of their surroundings and have an understanding of their duties towards it
- To get the children to feel comfortable expressing themselves in a debate

Resources

- A series of images: a tap with water coming out, a light switch, a light bulb, an open window, an open door

What to do

- Give a brief introduction explaining about the environment and how as individuals we can do things that help or hinder the environment.
- Show them the chart with two columns with good and bad for the environment.
- Take the children on a walk around part of the school, e.g. the bathroom.

- Ask them questions about the room, e.g. what are the lights for?
- Think about the tap. What is it for?
- Back in the classroom, show a picture, e.g. a light bulb and switch, and debate when it should be used
- Then ask, should we leave a tap running?
- Debate why or why not and whether it is good or bad.
- Ask the class if anyone has any other views.

Variations/extensions

- Ask them to think about their environment at home

Cross-curriculum links

- Humanities
- Science

Dealing with a feeling

> Some of the emotions we have are not ones we like. We all get them but it's how we deal with them that counts. This is a simple discussion based idea that encourages children to take the initiative when they are not feeling good.

Suitable for and curriculum fulfilment

- KS1
- Developing confidence and responsibility and making the most of their abilities
- To recognise, name and deal with their feelings in a positive way

Aims

- To recognise negative feelings
- To understand why they feel them
- To learn to think of simple plans to deal with them

Resources

- References:
  http://kidshealth.org/kid/feeling/emotion/anger.html
  http://www.phac-aspc.gc.ca/publicat/oes-bsu-02/child-eng.php
- Individual cards with single names of feelings and emotions written on them: sad / happy / angry / scared / surprise / anticipation / tired / excited
- Whiteboard

What to do

- Show the cards to the class.
- Explain that all these feelings are natural and everybody experiences them.
- Ask them to separate the feelings into two groups: feelings they like and feelings they don't like.

- Use the cards from the 'don't like' group (normally sad, angry, tired and scared).
- Ask why we feel these things.
- Explain that it is our body's way of telling us something.
- Write on the whiteboard and briefly talk about:
  - Angry – something we 'think' is unfair or wrong, has or is happening to us.
  - Sad – something not very nice has or is happening to us.
  - Tired – we need to rest or put more fuel in us.
  - Scared – something bad or something we do not like may happen to us.
- Discuss each feeling one at a time.
- Ask the class to give some examples of when they feel a certain way.
- Take each scenario and ask them to think what their body is telling them.
- Talk about how these feelings are natural and happen to all of us, and that it is important that we know how to deal with them when we feel that way.
- Discuss what can be done to help stop us feeling this way:
  - Stop, think and ask yourself, 'What is my body telling me?'
  - Take control and be proactive, e.g. talk to/get advice from someone you trust as soon as you can, take time out, walk away, go somewhere to calm down, change a routine.
  - Think about the possible outcome. Has the same thing happened before? Is there a pattern?
  - Think about what you can do to avoid it happening again.
- Recap that emotions are natural and nothing to be worried about as long as we know what we are feeling, why we are feeling it and how we can deal with it.

Variations/extensions

- Expand upon anger, discussing what we feel, why we feel it and techniques to deal with it: http://kidshealth.org/kid/feeling/emotion/anger.html

Cross-curriculum link

- Science

Feelings

To watch and participate in this short film and to give their responses in recognising the different emotions and feelings that result from different issues.

Suitable for and curriculum fulfilment

- KS1
- Developing confidence and responsibility and making the most of their abilities
- To recognise, name and deal with their feelings in a positive way

Aim

- To be able to express and recognise our emotions

Resource

- http://www.bbc.co.uk/scotland/education/health/feelings/ (Broadband version)

What to do

- Let the children watch the short movie which sets the scene and introduces them to the characters and scenarios.
- The children go on the journey through the park and have to decide what choices they want to make in response to the various scenarios they find themselves in.
- The children can work in small groups to make these decisions and at the end share them with the rest of the class.
- Encourage the children to stop and discuss the decisions they are making. Would they feel the same?
- Ask the children to share the decisions they have made and how their characters are feeling in the park.

Variations/extensions

- To role-play their own adventure through the park

Cross-curriculum link

- IT

How am I feeling?

To be able to deal with your emotions, you first need to be able to recognise them in yourself. This activity, based around charades, is a simple way to get children to recognise basic emotions.

Suitable for and curriculum fulfilment

- KS1
- Developing confidence and responsibility and making the most of their abilities
- To recognise, name and deal with their feelings in a positive way

Aims

- To recognise and name feelings
- To understand why we have feelings

Resources

- Individual cards with single names of feelings and emotions written on them: sad / happy / angry / scared / surprised / anticipation / tired / excited

What to do

- Ask how everyone is feeling today.
- Ask if they always feel that way.
- Talk briefly about how we can experience many different emotions and feelings, even in just one day.
- Show them a list of emotions and feelings.
- Ask a child to come to the front of the class and give them a card with one of these emotions or feelings written on it and ask them to act out the feeling using facial expression and body language.
- Ask the rest of the class to guess what emotion or feeling they are expressing.

- Ask the children to give examples of situations when they have felt that emotion or feeling.
- Repeat until all the cards have been acted out.
- Lay the cards out.
- Explain that all these emotions and feelings are our body's way of talking to us, e.g.
  - Why do we feel happy? ... We are feeling really good about ourselves.
  - Why do we feel sad? ... Something not very nice has happened or is happening to us.
  - Why do we feel anger? ... Something we think is unfair or wrong has or is happening to us.
  - Why do we feel excited? ... Something good is happening to us.
  - Why do we feel tired? ... We need to rest or eat something.
  - Why do we feel scared? ... Something bad or something we do not like may happen to us.
  - Why do we feel surprised? ... Something unusual/unexpected is happening to us.
  - Why do we feel anticipation? ... Something that will make us feel happy or sad could be about to happen.
- Explain that all these emotions and feelings are normal and are a part of life even if we do not like some as much as others.
- Explain that it is important that we know how we feel and understand why we feel like that.

Variations/extensions

- Ask the children to draw an outline of their body and to write all the emotions in them with an example of each one underneath

Cross-curriculum link

- Science

Mirror, mirror, on the wall

> This activity is to encourage the children to look more closely at facial expressions, both in themselves and other people.

Suitable for and curriculum fulfilment

- KS1
- Developing confidence and responsibility and making the most of their abilities
- To recognise, name and deal with their feelings in a positive way

Aim

- To help children recognise, both in themselves and in others, a range of expressions and emotions

Resources

- Mirrors
- Set of cards with different emotions written on them
- Whiteboard with images of faces

What to do

- Ask the children to sit in a circle or on the mat.
- Pointing to faces on the whiteboard, ask the children if they can identify the emotions.
- Ask the children when they might feel these emotions.
- Give each child a mirror.
- Explain that they are going to be shown an emotion written on a card and then they have to pretend to feel that way and look into the mirror to look at their face.
- Discuss their expressions.

- Pair the children off.
- Hand out the cards to the children face down.
- Ask them to take it in turns to make expressions based on what is written on their card while their partner has to guess the word on the card.
- Ask each child, with the use of a mirror, to draw their facial expression to depict an emotion.
- Ask each child to show the class their drawing and ask the class to guess the emotion they have drawn.

Variations/extensions

- Draw emotions of how we would feel, for example:
  - When we are opening presents
  - When we have done well in a test
  - When we ate something we didn't like

Cross-curriculum link

- Science

My special mix

> This activity is designed to get children to start thinking of what they like about themselves and think about what they are good at.

Suitable for and curriculum fulfilment

- KS1
- Developing confidence and responsibility and making the most of their abilities
- To think about themselves, learn from their experiences and recognise what they are good at

Aim

- To recognise what they feel are their strengths and their best qualities

Resource

- Whiteboard

What to do

- Ask the children to discuss and list all the qualities that they like and respect in each other and in other people they may know. They can be personality traits, skills or whatever they can think of, e.g. calm, kind, sharing, clever, funny, loyal, fast, strong, nice, well behaved, good at ... reading, football, swimming, singing, maths, dancing, etc.
- Write a list of these words on the whiteboard.
- Tell the children that they are going to make a special 'gingerbread kid' of themselves with only the best ingredients that make them who they are.

- Get them to draw a gingerbread character shape, cut it out with scissors and write their name at the top.
- Using the list on the whiteboard, ask the children to make up a recipe of all the things that make them special (they can add other qualities if they wish) and write them down on the body of the 'gingerbread kid'.
- Ask some of the children to come up and show their 'gingerbread kid' and talk about their qualities. Encourage them to say 'I am ...'

Variations/extensions

- Create a display in the classroom using all the gingerbread kids

Cross-curriculum links

- Literacy
- Art

What animal am I?

This activity is designed to get children to start thinking about what qualities they feel are their strengths by creating an animal that they feel reflects themselves.

Suitable for and curriculum fulfilment

- KS1
- Developing confidence and responsibility and making the most of their abilities
- To think about themselves, learn from their experiences and recognise what they are good at

Aim

- To think about themselves and their qualities

Resource

- Whiteboard with images of different animals with their descriptions

What to do

- Talk about different animals and how we attribute qualities to that animal.
- Talk about physical as well as emotional qualities, e.g.
  - cheetah – fast
  - fox – cunning
  - bear – strong
  - lion – brave, proud
  - beaver – industrious
  - penguin – cheery, optimistic
  - badger – inner strength, stubborn
  - mouse – sympathetic, kind, thoughtful
  - eagle – serious

- cat – curious
- meerkat – comical, funny
- dog – loyal, a good friend
- otter – agile, fun
- panda – peaceful
- peregrine falcon – fast, accurate
- spider – patient
- squirrel – athletic
- mole – bright
- rabbit – gentle
- elephant – good memory
- dolphin – sociable, playful, clever
- owl – wise, honest
- butterfly – beautiful, graceful
- bee/ant – hard working
- kangaroo – athletic, laid back
- koala – cute

- Ask them to think about what animal or animals they would be.
- Ask them to think about what they are good at or proud about and what they see as their strong points – for example, if one is good at football would they be an otter, falcon and a bear?
- Ask the children to create their own animal (that represents themselves) by either mixing and matching parts of these animals or by creating an imaginary animal from scratch.
- Ask them to list the qualities and what they relate to, e.g. good at football or a good friend.
- Ask them to show and tell the class about their animal, their qualities and how or why this reflects them.

Variations/extensions

- Make a mixed-up display using all the animals

Cross-curriculum links

- Art
- Literacy

A ladder

This activity is to get the class to create a simple goal chart.

Suitable for and curriculum fulfilment

- KS1
- Developing confidence and responsibility and making the most of their abilities
- To know how to set simple goals

Aim

- To learn how we can work together to attain our goals

Resource

- A paper ladder with five rungs

What to do

- Start this activity on a Monday.
- Ask the children to think about what the class goals are; they could be based on class rules:
  - Taking turns
  - Listening to each other
  - Lining up
  - Putting our hand up when we have a question
  - Finishing our work or tidying up.
- Agree as a class on one of these goals.
- Show the children a paper ladder with five rungs.
- Put at the top (the fifth rung) the agreed class goal.
- Write the name of the class on a piece of paper and get each child to write their name underneath.
- Stick it on the bottom rung (with movable low-tack tape or Blu-Tack).

- At the end of each day if we have reached our goal then we can move it up on the rung until we reach the top.
- By Friday we should have reached our goal and the children could be rewarded with an extra 5 minutes' golden time, or playtime.

Variations/extensions

- Think about goals they can attain at home

Cross-curriculum link

- Maths

Dominoes

> This is a quick little idea to understand that setting goals may need to include more manageable steps inbetween.

Suitable for and curriculum fulfilment

- KS1
- Developing confidence and responsibility and making the most of their abilities
- To know how to set simple goals

Aims

- To learn how to set simple goals with manageable steps
- To understand that these smaller steps are important and should be seen as mini goals to concentrate on in order to help reach the bigger goal

Resources

- A pack of dominoes
- An image of a small character to represent the child (maybe a picture stuck to a domino)
- An image of the item the child wishes to get (again stuck to a domino)

What to do

- Tell the children that you have set yourself a goal, e.g. it is to buy something. But there is a problem: it is a lot of money and you do not have enough.
- Place a domino at one end of the table and tell them this is you. Place another one at the other end to represent the item you want. Ask the class what you should do.
  Some suggestions:
  - Each week you could save some money.
  - How much can you save?

- How many weeks will it take to save the money? (A sum can be introduced here for the children to work out – I have x amount already, etc.)
- Slowly place a domino, which represents a week's savings, starting next to the domino representing you.
- Keep going until you have placed all the dominoes to represent all the weeks you need to save, making sure it reaches the goal.
- Talk about how you have made little goals, saving a certain amount every week, and how all these little goals add up to reaching the big goal.
- Knock the domino representing you and show how all those little goals reach the big one.

Variations/extensions

- This can be done with coins that are placed between a little character on one side and an image of the item on the other
- Ask the children to think about goals they have and discuss them in class and see how you can break them down into mini goals

Cross-curriculum link

- Maths

It's a goal!

To learn how to set simple goals by thinking and writing about what the children would like to achieve, how they can achieve it and how we can work to attain our goals.

Suitable for and curriculum fulfilment

- KS1
- Developing confidence and responsibility and making the most of their abilities
- To know how to set simple goals

Aim

- To learn how to set simple goals

Resources

- Whiteboard
- A piece of paper with an image of a football for each student (see Bespoke Resources)

What to do

- What are goals? Ask the children to think about goals and what they are.
  They could be anything from wanting to be a footballer or a ballet dancer, being able to sleep with the light off or saving to buy an expensive toy.
- Give each child a piece of paper with an outline of a football (they can cut this out).
- On a section of the ball, ask the children to write down their goal.
- Ask the children to think about how to attain this goal; encourage them to think about the specific steps they need to take in attaining this goal, almost like a journey, e.g.
  - Would they need to practise skills in the park and then join a football team? How many days each week would they need to practise?

- − Would they turn the bedroom light off and keep a hall light on and eventually turn that off?
- − Would they need to save up birthday money or pocket money? How many weeks do they need to save for?
- Every Monday they can fill in their football with anything they have done to make their goal more attainable.

Cross-curriculum links

- Literacy
- Maths
- IT

Bespoke resource

- See worksheet in Bespoke resources chapter at the end of the book

KS2
Ideas

Views

To give children the right language to be able to express their opinions including set phrases that are less confrontational and help encourage rather than hinder honest and positive discussions.

Suitable for and curriculum fulfilment

- KS2
- Developing confidence and responsibility and making the most of their abilities
- To talk and write about their opinions, and explain their views, on issues that affect themselves and society

Aim

- To help the children explain their opinions to others, be able to listen and exchange views, and be able to write about their opinions

Resource

- Whiteboard

What to do

- Give an example of how to express a view or an opinion, showing the best way to put across a point of view. The following are all good ways to start a discussion about your point of view:
  - In my view ...
  - In my opinion ...
  - From my point of view ...
  - From the point of view of ... (this would be used from the viewpoint of others)

- From their point of view ...

The following sentences express the position from which you are judging the situation:

- From my point of view it makes no difference if we go swimming or to the park.
- From the point of view of safety, you should always wear a helmet when you are on a bike.

• Ask the children to think of a sentence beginning with one of the above, where they can put across an opinion.

• Ask the children to think about other ways to start a sentence when giving an opinion:

- If you ask me ...
- To my mind ...
- As far as I am concerned ...

The following sentences might be used when you want to express an opinion that might be slightly critical or a stronger opinion or different from others:

- If you ask me, they should have better school lunches.
- To my mind we spend far too much time on homework.
- As far as I am concerned the matter is over with.

• Ask the children again to think of a simple sentence starting with one of the above.

• Talk to the children about alternatives that they could use in their writing to express an opinion:

- I think that ...
- It seems to me that ...
- I believe that ...
- I do not agree that ...

• Ask the children to think about how they would write their opinions to this question:

- Should animals be kept in zoos?

• Think of the following words we could use to link our thoughts in more detail:

- That is to say ...
- By this I mean ...
- To be more precise ...

Variations/extensions

- Working in pairs, one child gives their opinion arguing for something and the other child argues against

Cross·curriculum link

- Literacy

My opinion

Is there too much traffic on the road? To be able to discuss and write about their opinions on traffic and how it affects them and other people in the community.

Suitable for and curriculum fulfilment

- KS2
- Developing confidence and responsibility and making the most of their abilities
- To talk and write about their opinions, and explain their views, on issues that affect themselves and society

Aims

- To help the children to think about their opinions and how to express them verbally and on paper
- To explore and discuss a topic which affects their local area

Resources

- Whiteboard
- Map of local area showing roads, traffic lights and road signals (these can be added)

What to do

- Ask the children to think about what issues affect themselves and society (by society we mean everyone).
- What makes up road traffic?
  - Why do we have it? What are its uses?
  - What are the pros and cons of traffic?
  - Is the balance right?
  - If not, what should the balance be?

- Ask the children to think about the local bus services and train services.
  - Should there be more public transportation?
- Are there any bike lanes?
  - Should there be more bike lanes?
- Next ask the children to write a list expressing their views on how they would change traffic in their local area.
  - Encourage them also to think about how, for example, local business could be affected.
- Ask them to share their opinions with the class.

Variations/extensions

- Get a local map and place a cross marking the school on the map. Then children are to find where they live and mark it on the map. How does each child get to school? After this, ask them how they would change the road layout of the map. Would they have more zebra crossings, more bike lanes?

Cross-curriculum link

- Humanities

Interviews

To listen to two famous authors talk about their achievements.

Suitable for and curriculum fulfilment

- KS2
- Developing confidence and responsibility and making the most of their abilities
- To recognise their worth as individuals by identifying positive things about themselves and their achievements, seeing their mistakes, making amends and setting personal goals

Aim

- To be able to see how other people have achieved their goals and for the children to see how they can attain their goals by identifying positive things about themselves

Resources

- http://www.bbc.co.uk/scotland/learning/authorslive/michael_morpurgo/
- http://www.bbc.co.uk/scotland/learning/authorslive/jacqueline_wilson/
- A collection of books by the authors

What to do

Before the lesson the teacher should listen and maybe choose different parts of the interview to listen to or watch, as each of the interviews is approximately 40 minutes long.

- First, before listening to the interviews, ask the children if they have read any of Michael Morpurgo's or Jacqueline Wilson's books.
  - Which of the books have they read?
- Show some of their books and pass them around.
- Next, listen to their interviews.

- Ask the children if they know what inspired the authors when they were young.
- What are the authors' achievements?
- Did they have goals when they were children?
- Have they made any mistakes?

Variations/extensions

- Ask the children to think about their goals and to write them down

Cross-curriculum link

- Literacy

Superheroes

To design a superhero putting all their own strengths and achievements into a cartoon strip; also using this cartoon strip to show their mistakes and how their superhero can put these right.

Suitable for and curriculum fulfilment

- KS2
- Developing confidence and responsibility and making the most of their abilities
- To recognise their worth as individuals by identifying positive things about themselves and their achievements, seeing their mistakes, making amends and setting personal goals

Aim

- To be able to identify what they are good at, what their mistakes are and how to improve upon them

Resources

- Whiteboard
- Comic books

What to do

- First let the children look at some comic books.
- Tell them to pay close attention to a superhero.
- Does a superhero always have strengths?
  - What are these strengths?
  - What strengths do you have?

- Ask the children to think about how to design a superhero based upon themselves with their own strengths.
  - Remind the children these strengths do not have to be physical – for example, good at reading is a strength.
  - Listening to our friends is a strength.
- Get them to think about a very simple comic strip.
- Show them how to draw boxes and speech bubbles.
- Ask them to divide the page into nine boxes.
- For now only fill in three boxes showing their strengths.
- Explain that with speech bubbles they could be telling someone else about their strengths.
- Then with the further three boxes show what their achievements are.
- With the next two empty boxes think about something they have done that they would like to change.
- Then in the final remaining box think carefully about something they want to achieve.
  Show this as something they want to be able to achieve or to make amends.

Variations/extensions

- To design a shield with all their strengths written on it

Cross-curriculum links

- Art
- Literacy

How does your garden grow?

To face a new challenge of making a school garden. To work together and to make the right choices to be able to achieve this.

Suitable for and curriculum fulfilment

- KS2
- Developing confidence and responsibility and making the most of their abilities
- To face new challenges positively by collecting information, looking for help, making responsible choices and taking action

Aims

- To feel confident when doing something for the first time
- To face new challenges
- To know how to ask for help and where to look for help

Resources

- Whiteboard
- Various garden equipment and seeds (the children first need to decide what is needed)

What to do

- Explain to the children that gardens are very significant for protecting biodiversity (explain what this means) in the UK and can be a refuge for wildlife.
- How can we maximise the potential of the grounds of the school to become a garden?
- Who can we get involved? School gardens can provide an environment in which students, teachers and parents can be involved.

- Ask the children to consider the following framework:
  - Form a garden committee, by looking at anyone from our community whom we can ask for help (a gardener, someone who works at a garden centre, a parent).
  - Think about how we can raise money for our garden.
  - What is the purpose of the garden – is it to grow vegetables, plants?
- Together, walk around the school grounds and choose a permanent garden site.
  - Remind the children that it needs to be in an area that receives plenty of sunlight, has good drainage and is accessible to students and teachers.
- Decide which roles the children are going to have in the planning and planting of the garden.
  - Make sure every child has a part in the garden.
  - Who is going to be designing the garden?
  - Who is going to be planting the seeds?
  - Who is going to be watering the garden?
  - Who is going to be weeding the garden?

Variations/extensions

- To find out information about flower shows. Can they grow something to enter? They will have to find out the information, get the application forms, etc.

Cross-curriculum links

- Literacy
- Science

Paws

Hold a day at school as a 'paw' day. Find out about guide dogs and how they help; understand what it is like to be blind and to face challenges positively. Order a pack with posters and whiteboard materials.

Suitable for and curriculum fulfilment

- KS2
- Developing confidence and responsibility and making the most of their abilities
- To face new challenges positively by collecting information, looking for help, making responsible choices and taking action

Aim

- To understand the challenges faced by blind and partially sighted people, and how people can overcome these difficulties and lead independent lives

Resources

- http://www.guidedogs.org.uk/index.php?id=225
- Order a pack about guide dogs for schools (from the above website)
- Register and invite a speaker into your class

What to do

- Ask the children if they know what a guide dog does.
- Do they know anyone who has a guide dog?
- You can invite along a speaker (and maybe a dog or puppy).
- After the children have listened to the speaker, encourage questions.
- Look at the school pack and ask the children to collect information on how they can raise money or help.
- Encourage the children to understand what it is like to be blind, the challenges they face.
- Ask the children to make posters and leaflets to inform the rest of the school.

Variations/extensions

- To produce a school assembly on how the whole school can help in a fund-raising activity

Cross-curriculum links

- Literacy
- IT (to make the posters and leaflets)

Marking time

To design a timeline aimed at making children aware of puberty and that this is a natural part of the growing-up process.

Suitable for and curriculum fulfilment

- KS2
- Developing confidence and responsibility and making the most of their abilities
- To recognise, as they approach puberty, how people's emotions change at that time and how to deal with their feelings towards themselves, their family and others in a positive way

Aims

- To understand that puberty is a natural part of our lives
- To know it includes emotional changes as well

Resource

- Teacher to make their own timeline first to show the children

What to do

- The teacher to show their timeline, explaining what a timeline is.
- Show where the key milestones have been marked.
- Ask the children to start their own timeline (some of this information they will have to find out at home and can bring in pictures).
- Ask the children to mark on it key milestones in their lives. For example:
  - When they got their first teeth
  - When they walked
  - When they talked
  - First day at school
  - First tooth fell out

- Given pocket money, etc.
- Given certain responsibilities.
- Ask them to add a couple of things they will do in the future:
  - Go to secondary school
  - When they might be old enough to drive
  - Go to university
  - Have a boyfriend/girlfriend
  - Get a job.
- Once their timeline has been completed, discuss the different milestones.
- Then talk about how part of growing up includes puberty and this is something that happens to all of us along this timeline, at slightly different times from each other.
- Ask if the children have heard of puberty and if they have any idea what it is.
  - It is a natural and essential part of our timeline (growing-up process).
- Discuss what puberty is and how it affects us physically.
- Talk about where on the timeline puberty takes place (but that it takes place at slightly different times).
- Explain that we not only change physically but also emotionally.
- Talk about some of these emotions and how each change takes time to adjust to.

Variations/extensions

- Continue with the timeline

Cross-curriculum links

- Maths
- Science
- IT

Taking control

To make a poster showing how to take control of your emotions and feelings.

Suitable for and curriculum fulfilment

- KS2
- Developing confidence and responsibility and making the most of their abilities
- To recognise, as they approach puberty, how people's emotions change at that time and how to deal with their feelings towards themselves, their family and others in a positive way

Aim

- To feel in control of their emotions and feelings during puberty

Resources

- A3 paper
- Whiteboard

What to do

- Talk to the children about puberty from the viewpoint of their emotions and feelings. Explain that, even though they might at times feel out of control, it is possible to feel more in control.
- Ask the children to think about how they can take control of their emotions and feelings.
  - Do they think all their friends experience mood changes?
- Try to think of strategies that could help them control their emotions. For example:
  - Trying to count to 10 when you feel yourself losing your temper.
  - Separating yourself from a situation where you don't feel in control.

- Encourage the children to look at the situation from another point of view.
- Suggest talking to friends; you are not alone!
  - Talking to parents, they have been through it!
- Exercise as much as you can (produces more beta-endorphin, a hormone that controls stress and improves mood).
- Get enough sleep; when you are tired it is hard to make clear judgements.
- There is nothing wrong if you feel like crying.
- Have patience: your mood can change just as quickly as it started.
- Ask the children to choose some of the above points and to design a poster (working together in groups). The title of the poster should be TAKE CONTROL.

Variations/extensions

- To role-play in groups of two, one to be the child, the other a parent
- To create different situations

Cross-curriculum links

- Science
- Art
- IT

An object

> The children ask their parents to lend them something (or a photograph) from their work and briefly write about their job and how they use that object at work.

Suitable for and curriculum fulfilment

- KS2
- Developing confidence and responsibility and making the most of their abilities
- To learn about the range of jobs carried out by people they know, and to understand how they can develop skills to make their own contribution in the future

Aim

- To find out how different people contribute to the community and to have a better understanding of skills needed for different jobs

Resources

- Different objects (or photo of it) supplied by parents from their workplace
- Ask the parent to write a brief summary of their job to go with it

What to do

- Have a quick talk about the range of jobs people can do. Think about the most varied.
- Choose an object that a child has brought in from their parent's work.
- Ask the children if they can guess the job.
- Ask if the child who brought in the object or photo wants to tell the class what it is used for and what their parent does. If not, read out the description. (Some objects might be easier to guess than others.)

- Continue with different objects and different jobs.
- Ask the children to think about what job they would like to have in the future.
  - To think about what skills they have, what they like doing, what their interests are.

Variations/extensions

- Dress-up day: Everyone to dress up or bring an object for a career day at school

Cross-curriculum link

- Literacy

Different options, different ways

This activity is about understanding there is a vast number of different jobs and these require different kinds of training.

Suitable for and curriculum fulfilment

- KS2
- Developing confidence and responsibility and making the most of their abilities
- To learn about the range of jobs carried out by people they know, and to understand how they can develop skills to make their own contribution in the future

Aim

- To learn about the variety of jobs and how they require different kinds and levels of training

Resource

- http://learnenglishkids.britishcouncil.org/en/fun-with-english/job-mixer

What to do

- Ask the children to think about what they would like to be when they are grown up.
- Ask the children to talk to five grown-ups they know (mums, dads, uncles, aunts, neighbours, friend's parents, etc). They can do this by email, phone or in person.
  Get them to ask three questions:
  - What job do you do?
  - What did you need to do to be able to do the job? (They can tick more than one box.)
    - ☐ Training college
    - ☐ University
    - ☐ City and Guilds

☐ Apprenticeship (taught on the job by mentors)
☐ Learn at home and pass exams
☐ Start straight from school and learn on the job
– Is it important to be continually learning to do the job? If so, why?

In class on the whiteboard categorise the jobs into groups based on the paths above taken to achieve them.
Ask if they can think of any other jobs that may fit into each category.
Discuss the last question.

Variations/extensions

- You can add the number of years of formal training required to the list as well as degree, Masters, PhD and Doctorate

Cross-curriculum links

- Literacy
- Maths
- IT

My career

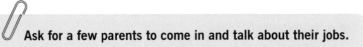

Ask for a few parents to come in and talk about their jobs.

Suitable for and curriculum fulfilment

- KS2
- Developing confidence and responsibility and making the most of their abilities
- To learn about the range of jobs carried out by people they know, and to understand how they can develop skills to make their own contribution in the future

Aims

- To find out how different people contribute to the community
- To have a better understanding of skills needed for different jobs

Resource

- Parents!

What to do

- Before beginning it is important that parents have a brief outline of how to present what they do.
- These are suggestions for the outline of a presentation by a parent:
    - What they wanted to do when they were young.
    - What qualifications they needed for their job.
    - What their career path has been. (What other jobs have they done?)
    - What they do now.
    - What it involves.
- Encourage the children to listen and only to ask questions at the end.

Variations/extensions

- To find out about different jobs that people do around the school. To visit the kitchen and talk to the staff about their jobs, go into the office and talk to the head, deputy head and secretary

Cross-curriculum link

- Literacy

It's a game!

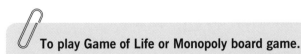

To play Game of Life or Monopoly board game.

Suitable for and curriculum fulfilment

- KS2
- Developing confidence and responsibility and making the most of their abilities
- To look after their money and realise that future wants and needs may be met through saving

Aim

- To understand about sources of money, how to use it and the value of saving

Resources

- Monopoly
- Game of Life
  (Ask the children to bring in either Monopoly or Game of Life if they have it)

What to do

- Game of Life encourages you to go around the board, making choices about life, which involves the money you earn.
- Monopoly makes you think about how to buy but also how to save for houses or to pay rent to someone else. (With Monopoly I would use the quick version of the game.)
- Put children in groups for both games. Ideally have at least two sets of each game (four in total).
- Put a time limit on the game.
- Plenary
  - Discuss what the class has learnt from playing.
  - Do we have to plan what we do with our money?
  - Do we have to save some of our money?

Variations/extensions

- Make up your own board game: Using the concepts of money, saving, spending and investing make up a very simple game

Cross-curriculum link

- Maths

Money dilemmas

To have different scenarios where children have to think about how to save and how to manage their pocket money.

Suitable for and curriculum fulfilment

- KS2
- Developing confidence and responsibility and making the most of their abilities
- To look after their money and realise that future wants and needs may be met through saving

Aim

- To understand the importance of money management and ways to save

Resource

- Whiteboard

What to do

- Ask the children if they think parents should give children pocket money once a week, once a month or every day.
- In small groups discuss what they think would be better for saving and managing money.
- Then ask the children to report back on their findings.
- Now write down how they do (or would) spend their pocket money. Is it on toys, sweets, snacks, entertainment, birthday presents for family and friends?
- Also think about saving:
  - How much would they save? Where would they save it?

(Explain to the children that they should try to save 10 per cent or 20 per cent of their pocket money.)

Variations/extensions

- Ask the children to write down everything they spend their money on, including bus fares, sweets, presents, snacks, etc.

Cross-curriculum links

- Literacy
- IT

Pocket money

To watch a video about how a boy spends his allowance (pocket money) and the decisions he makes.

Suitable for and curriculum fulfilment

- KS2
- Developing confidence and responsibility and making the most of their abilities
- To look after their money and realise that future wants and needs may be met through saving

Aim

- To understand about sources of money, how to use it and the value of saving

Resource

- http://www.youtube.com/watch?v=GawH48QNDfc

What to do

- Let the children watch the video (it uses dollars).
- The song teaches about budgeting your money.
- It teaches about the expenses people encounter and ways to save money.
- When the children have watched the video, ask the following questions:
  - Do you think that at the beginning he spent his pocket money wisely?
  - What other expenses do you think he might have encountered?
  - At the end do you think he managed his pocket money well?
  - Do you get any pocket money?
  - How do you spend it?
  - Do you save?

Variations/extensions

- Ask the children to do a week chart (like in the video) and to work out what they can spend each day and how long it would take to save for a bike

Cross-curriculum link

- Maths

Chapter 2

Preparing to play an active role as citizens

Introduction

Some of the following activities can be used for KS1 and KS2 but it is really for the teacher to use their discretion knowing the ability of their class.

There are twenty areas that need to be covered in KS1 and KS2 in this chapter. All the activities have been laid out following this order and below each title is a full description of which one it relates to.

Key Stage 1

During Key Stage 1 children are encouraged to look beyond themselves and to begin to see how they fit into, affect and should behave in their respective and collective communities and environments. There are nine main areas that need to be covered:

- To know how to take part in discussions with one other person and the whole class
- To be able to take part in a simple debate about topical issues
- To recognise choices that they can make, and recognise the difference between right and wrong
- To know how to reach an agreement and follow rules for their group and classroom, and understand how rules help them
- To realise that people and other living things have needs, and that they have responsibilities to meet them
- To know that they belong to various groups and communities, such as family and school
- To know what improves and harms their local, natural and built environments and about some of the ways people look after them
- To contribute to the life of the class and school
- To realise that money comes from different sources and can be used for different purposes.

Key Stage 2

As children increasingly become aware of the world around them, Key Stage 2 begins to build on the earlier themes as well as introduce more complex ideas as diverse as democracy, spiritual welfare, multi-culturalism and how we are presented with information that can influence who we are and what we think. By the end of Key Stage 2 pupils should have covered the following eleven areas:

- To research, discuss and debate topical issues, problems and events
- To know why and how rules and laws are made and enforced, why different rules are needed in different situations and how to take part in making and changing rules

- To realise the consequences of anti-social and aggressive behaviours, such as bullying and racism, on individuals and communities
- To understand that there are different kinds of responsibilities, rights and duties at home, at school and in the community, and that these can sometimes conflict with each other
- To reflect on spiritual, moral, social and cultural issues, using imagination to understand other people's experiences
- To resolve differences by looking at alternatives, making decisions and explaining choices
- To know what democracy is, and about the basic institutions that support it locally and nationally
- To recognise the role of voluntary, community and pressure groups
- To appreciate the range of national, regional, religious and ethnic identities in the United Kingdom
- To understand that resources can be allocated in different ways and these economic choices affect individuals, communities and the sustainability of the environment
- To explore how the media present information.

KS1

Ideas

Lemons

This is for older KS1 children or KS2.

To role-play in groups and then to discuss their findings with the whole class.

Discussion and role-play are always good in PSHE. They encourage children to think through and reason. In this role-play there is an interesting alternative, which can only come about with discussion.

Suitable for and curriculum fulfilment

- KS1
- Preparing to play an active role as citizens
- To know how to take part in discussions with one other person and the whole class

Aims

- To give children an understanding of how important it is to:
  - Listen to what the other person says
  - Try to find ways to co-operate
  - Use all available information
  - Look at situations from different angles

Resources

- Lemons
- Two sets of recipe cards for:
  Lemonade
  Ingredients: 1 cup of water, juice from 1 lemon, 5 ice cubes
  - Squeeze the juice from 1 lemon and throw away the skin (rind)
  - Using HALF a lemon's juice is not enough
  - Add 1 cup of water
  - Add the 5 ice cubes

Lemon cake
Ingredients: 1 cup of flour, skin (rind) from 1 lemon, 2 eggs
- Grate or chop up the skin (rind) of 1 lemon, throw away the inside bit
- Using HALF the lemon skin (rind) is not enough
- Mix the flour, eggs and lemon skin (rind) together
- Bake in oven

What to do

- Set the scene: Mum and Dad are at home and they both need a lemon but there is only one lemon left in the fridge. They both have recipes that require a lemon. One needs the lemon to make lemonade; the other needs the lemon to make a lemon cake. What should they do?
- Divide the class into pairs or pairs of groups and give one pair one recipe and the other pair the other recipe. Tell them to read their recipe carefully to the other group and then to role-play and discuss what should be done.
- Give the children 5 minutes to discuss what they should do.
- Ask the children to write down their solution.
- Ask the children to read out their solutions.
- By cutting the lemon in half there won't be enough to make the lemonade or the lemon cake.

After discussion they should have found a way to share the lemon, as one parent needs only the juice and the other only the rind.

Variations/extensions

- Ask the children to make up their own scenarios when they need to negotiate and compromise

Cross-curriculum link

- Drama

Pass the conch

> One of the first steps in taking part in a discussion is letting the other person speak, listening to and understanding what they are saying.

Suitable for and curriculum fulfilment

- KS1
- Preparing to play an active role as citizens
- To be able to take part in a simple debate about topical issues

Aim

- To get the children to take part in a discussion that they are passionate about but have the discipline to listen to the other person, understand what they are saying and counter with an appropriate response in a polite, non-antagonistic fashion

Resources

- An item that the child has to hold when they speak – the 'conch' or whatever name you wish to call it. This can be a beanbag, a soft ball or a hat that can be gently thrown or passed between one another
- Whiteboard

What to do

- Have a list of topics to discuss, e.g. different football teams, players, TV programmes, musicians, personalities, famous people in history or something that is relevant to the particular lesson.
- Find two children who are passionate about the same thing but have different views.
- Ask them to discuss why, for example, their football team is the best.
- Explain that this is as much about how you discuss the topic as it is about who has the best points of view.

- Write the rules on the whiteboard:
  - To speak only when holding the 'conch'
  - To sit up straight
  - To always be polite
  - To be respectful of the other person's opinion (don't mock or laugh).
- Encourage the children to use phrases like:
  - I believe ...
  - I think ...
  - I disagree because ...
  - In my opinion ...
- Ask the children to listen to what the other person says and, where possible, to counter their view based on what they have heard, before moving on to other points, e.g. 'So and so is good at scoring goals' with 'but so and so has scored more goals.'
- Guide them through the process where needed.
- Stop the discussion where appropriate to talk about respectfulness, interrupting and general politeness and etiquette (including body language).
- Ask the class who they thought was the more polite based on the rules on the whiteboard.
- Repeat with two other children and so on.

Variations/extensions

- This can also be carried out with the whole class in a circle passing the 'conch' around with a discussion that they can all take part in
- This can be used as part of discussions about History, Literature or as a basis for Drama

Cross·curriculum links

- History
- Literature
- Drama

Pros and cons

Debating is about seeing both sides of an argument as well as thinking, reasoning, listening and maintaining concentration. This game includes all of these without being a straightforward debate. It can be as long or as short as required. It is also a good way to 'warm up' the class for some role-play involving different points of view.

Suitable for and curriculum fulfilment

- KS1
- Preparing to play an active role as citizens
- To be able to take part in a simple debate about topical issues

Aims

- To encourage the children to think of both sides of a topic
- To get the children to think and reason quickly
- To get the children to listen to other people (both the teacher and the other children)

Resources

- Cards with subjects written on them to hand out to the children
  There should be two cards for each subject, one with 'A good thing about ... is ...' and one with 'A bad thing about ... is ...'
  Subjects should have easy to think of pros and cons, e.g. fast food, staying up late, winter, rain, homework, traffic, sweets. They can be based on current topics you have been doing in class, used for revisiting topics or just general things (see Bespoke Resources)

What to do

- Hand out the subject cards randomly round the circle.
- Give the children a short moment to think of one thing that supports the sentence on their card.
- Call out the first topic, e.g. fast food.
- Ask two children to stand.
  - The first child asked to speak is the one who has 'A good thing about … is …' Ask them to say the sentence and finish it with one reason.
  - The second child then says their sentence with their reason
- Call out the next topic.
- When everyone has had a turn, get the children to swap their card with someone else and repeat as many times as you feel is appropriate.
- With odd numbers in the class the teacher can take part.
- Depending on the group this can be fun when there is some sense of escalating pace involved.

Variations/extensions

- If the class is good at this game the next stage is to tell them they cannot repeat a reason that has already been given

Cross-curriculum links

- Literacy
- Drama

Bespoke resource

- See ready to cut out cards in Bespoke resources chapter at the end of the book

Putting yourself on the line

This activity is a fun way to encourage children to participate in thinking about and discussing what their views and opinions are. This can be used to go over other areas of PSHE either to refresh their memories or to introduce new topics.

Suitable for and curriculum fulfilment

- KS1
- Preparing to play an active role as citizens
- To be able to take part in a simple debate about topical issues

Aims

- To feel comfortable expressing themselves in a debate
- To start to think about things in a less black and white manner

Resources

- A line:
  - A long piece of string stretched between two chairs
- Something to fix their drawings on to the line: Blu-Tack, pegs or paper clips. At one end have 'Agree', in the middle 'It Depends' and 'Don't Agree' at the other end
- Statement examples (these are to create discussion so there may be some grey areas):
  - It is important that I do what adults tell me to do
  - I need to be clean to be healthy so I need to have a bath every night
  - I should never eat sweets because they are unhealthy
  - I should never push someone away
  - My friend stays up late every night; I should always be allowed to stay up late as well
  - My parents should let me do whatever I want
  - Homework is not important
  - It's always safe to cross at a zebra crossing
  - I should spend all my pocket money every week

What to do

- Ask each child to draw a silhouette picture of themselves with their name clearly written in the middle.
- While the children are doing this create your line with the signs.
- Tell the children you are going to read out some statements and they have to decide what they feel and think about it.
- If they really strongly agree they should hang their character at the 'Agree' end; if they agree a little bit but not completely then somewhere between the 'Agree' and 'It Depends', etc.
- Give the children an example, especially one that explains the middle area:
  - It is important that you do what adults tell you to do.
- Talk through some reasoning:
  - It's important to listen to adults.
  - But adults can be strangers as well as people you trust.
  - It also depends on what they tell you to do.
- If they think there are reasons where you cannot completely agree then the character goes somewhere in the middle of the line.
- Read out another statement and give them a few moments to think about it.
- Ask the children to come up and attach their drawing on to the line then to sit down again.
- Ask different children why they decided to put their character where they did.
- Have a discussion.
- If the children feel that they have changed their minds ask them to come up and move their drawing. If they feel the same then they should stay seated.
- If some of the children move their drawings ask why they changed their opinion.
- Repeat with another statement.

Variations/extensions

- If you have enough room, ask the children to come and stand on a line on the floor where they think shows how they feel about a statement

Cross-curriculum link

- Literacy

Stand up!

> This activity is a way to engage children in debate. It can be used as a starting point to go on to discuss other areas in PSHE and some other areas of the curriculum.

Suitable for and curriculum fulfilment

- KS1
- Preparing to play an active role as citizens
- To be able to take part in a simple debate about topical issues

Aims

- To consider other children's situations
- To learn to express opinions and views
- To understand the difference between 'needs' and 'wants'
- To collectively create a basic children's Human Rights bill

Resources

- Beanbag
- Whiteboard
- Websites for reference:
  http://www.direct.gov.uk/en/Parents/ParentsRights/DG_4003313
  http://www.liberty-human-rights.org.uk/human-rights/human-rights/index.php

What to do

- Sit the class in a circle and explain the rule that anyone who wants to speak has to be holding the beanbag. Each child must throw the beanbag back to the teacher as soon as they have finished speaking.
- Tell the children about the topic of Human Rights and explain that they are going to form their own set of rules for how children should be treated.
- Start to talk about the basic reasons for Human Rights. Ask questions.
- Agree to various points during the discussion by having a vote, with those who agree standing up and saying 'yes'.
- Write a list of things agreed on the whiteboard.
- Ask the children to present their bill of rights to the school assembly.

Cross-curriculum links

- PSHE 1a, 1b, 2a, 2c, 2d, 2e
- History
- Geography

A good person

A simple 'right' or 'wrong' game that gets the children expressing their views, discussing and understanding the concept of voting.

Suitable for and curriculum fulfilment

- KS1
- Preparing to play an active role as citizens
- To recognise choices that they can make, and recognise the difference between right and wrong

Aims

- To learn to discuss and agree on subjects, working together to achieve a common goal
- To recognise the differences between right and wrong

Resources

- Short situations written on individual cards where the action of the person was either right or wrong (e.g. at lunch I ate up all my vegetables; yesterday I hit my little brother/sister)
- Two pieces of paper can be two colours, one for 'right' and one for 'wrong', for each child

What to do

- Ask the children to write a very big 'right' on one of the pieces of paper and a big 'wrong' on the other.
- Ask a child to come to the front and read out one of the 'situation' cards to the rest of the class.
- Ask the rest of the class to discuss. Rather than come to any conclusions, just get their ideas and positions on the issue.

- Have a vote, where each child holds up either the 'right' or the 'wrong' or keeps their cards down if they are not sure.
- Ask a child to count up how many votes for 'right' and how many for 'wrong'.
- Discuss the result.

Variations/extensions

- This activity can be made more specific by narrowing it down to what makes a good friend (KS1 4a: How behaviour affects others), how to be good to yourself (KS1 3a: Healthy eating), how to look after the environment, peer pressure, etc.

Cross-curriculum link

- Drama

Good advice

> Puppets can be a great way to engage children as well as tackle issues that can be too sensitive to deal with directly. This activity is about recognising right from wrong as well as exploring the reasons. It is also about encouraging children to feel free to speak openly and to feel confident to play a part in the lesson.

Suitable for and curriculum fulfilment

- KS1
- Preparing to play an active role as citizens
- To recognise choices that they can make, and recognise the difference between right and wrong

Aims

- To make decisions about right and wrong
- To give the children a position of responsibility and empowerment
- To discuss in a group

Resources

- A puppet
- Box turned into a TV set if desired
- Card that is the same size as the TV screen with the title of the show on one side and 'to be continued ...' on the other
- A short list of dilemmas that have varied outcomes, e.g. sometimes the puppet did the wrong thing, sometimes the right thing or hasn't yet done anything and needs advice on what to do (this can be taped to the back of the box)

What to do

- Tell the children they are going to see a new TV show.
- Remove the title of the show from the screen to reveal the puppet.
- The puppet introduces him/herself.
- The puppet tells his/her dilemma and asks the children for advice.
- If the puppet made the wrong choice get the puppet to ask, 'What should I have done?'
- Discuss with the class.

Variations/extensions

- Have a character who is the villain of the show talk to the children about what he/she has been up to. Tell the children that every time the villain says something bad they should put their hand up, or if you don't mind the noise, call out 'Booo'. Discuss each one

Cross-curriculum link

- Art

Questions of right or wrong

This activity is based around questions that children should consider before making choices and decisions.

Suitable for and curriculum fulfilment

- KS1
- Preparing to play an active role as citizens
- To recognise choices that they can make, and recognise the difference between right and wrong

Aim

- To introduce some questions to the children that will help them make appropriate choices

Resources

- List of questions up on the whiteboard:
  - Is it dangerous (to you or someone or something else)?
  - Could you get into trouble if you did this?
  - Would it be bad if everyone did this?
  - Will it upset or hurt anyone?
  - Would your parents or teacher be upset with you if you did this?
- List of scenarios on cards, e.g.
  - Throw your litter on the floor
  - Say sorry to your friend
  - Go to the cinema
  - Take something that isn't yours
  - Wash your hands after going to the toilet
  - Play football in the road
  - Call someone names
  - Kick someone
  - Help your mum or dad around the house
  - Do your homework (always a good one to do just before you hand it out to them!)

What to do

- Ask a child to come to the front of the class.
- Give the child a scenario that only they are allowed to read.
- Get the class, one child at a time, to ask a question from the list on the whiteboard to the child at the front.
- If the child answers 'yes' to any of the questions, the child who asked the question shouts out ...'DON'T DO IT!'
- If the child answers 'no' to all the questions then the class can shout out ...'DO IT!'
- Ask the child to reveal what the scenario was and discuss.
- This is about getting the children to remember the questions. Discuss the questions and talk about how, if they stop to think, these can help them make good decisions.
- Ask the children if there are any more questions they could ask and add them to the list.

Cross-curriculum link

- Drama

A pledge

How belonging to a group makes us stronger, in this case working together as a class.

Suitable for and curriculum fulfilment

- KS1
- Preparing to play an active role as citizens
- To know how to reach an agreement and follow rules for their group and classroom, and understand how rules help them

Aim

- To get the children to agree on their class rules

Resources

- Coloured piece of card
- Finger paint

What to do

- Ask the children to think about rules that help us in the class.
- Help them with the words (if necessary): Listen, Take turns, Put your hand up, etc.
- Write the children's answers on the whiteboard.
- Ask the class – Why do we need rules?
- Ask the children to write down some of the rules that they think are important (if necessary copying from the whiteboard) on a piece of white paper.
- Choose one rule from each child.
- Ask the children to cut out and stick them on to the coloured card.
- Ask them to give their pledge to do their best to follow these rules by putting their thumbprint on the coloured card and writing their name next to it.
- Place the poster up on a wall where it is easily visible.

Variations/extensions

- Discuss rules that are needed in different situations, e.g. the swimming pool, the kitchen, a place of work (building site), on the road

Cross-curriculum links

- Literacy
- Art

Chaos in class

This is a simple and fun way to show why rules are needed in class and can be used as a starting point to discuss and create class rules. By getting the children to act out being a class of strong personalities that have disruptive traits, it allows them to think about how their actions can make a difference. This can be noisy!

Suitable for and curriculum fulfilment

- KS1
- Preparing to play an active role as citizens
- To know how to reach an agreement and follow rules for their group and classroom, and understand how rules help them

Aims

- To get the children to see what a class could be like without rules
- To see that there are many different things that can disrupt the class
- To discuss why rules can be good

Resources

- Pieces of card with names of different characters for half of the class: Mr Stand-up-sit-down, Miss Wriggly, Mr Laugh-a-lot, Miss Tap-Tap, Mr Noisy, Miss Poke, Miss Clap-Clap, Mr Hum, Miss Sing-song, Mr Giggle, Miss Miaow-Miaow, Mr Bark, etc. There can be more than one of each card
- Write a brief description of what to do under the name on each card

What to do

- Give a card to every other child.
- Ask them to act out what is on the card when you say 'go' and to stop and sit still when you say 'stop'.

- All those without cards must sit still, behave and listen.
- Start talking to the class about rules.
- Tell the children that you want them to write down some words as you say them.
- Indicate to those with cards to act out their characters. (Say 'go'.)
- Continue saying the words you want the children to write down, without raising your voice.
- When you feel the point has been made say stop, sit everyone down and discuss.
- Ask the children to stand up and tell the class what they wrote.
- Ask why they didn't write all the words down.
- Ask the children not given cards how it felt trying to be taught when all the noise was going on.
- Discuss and create a series of class rules.

Cross-curriculum link

- Drama

Blooming kids

This activity uses the analogy of a flower to reflect what we need as humans to become a balanced and happy person able to reach our potential.

Suitable for and curriculum fulfilment

- KS1
- Preparing to play an active role as citizens
- To realise that people and other living things have needs, and that they have responsibilities to meet them

Aim

- To introduce to the children the idea that we have a variety of needs both emotional and physical that help us develop into balanced and happy people

Resources

- Coloured paper
- Scissors
- Glue
- Large sheet of paper

What to do

- Talk to the class about flowers and what flowers need to survive, grow and blossom to their full potential, e.g. regular feeding (water or rain), protection when a small shoot, nutrition and sunshine.
- Mention how all living plants need these things.
- Draw a line across the large sheet of paper and draw a seed in the ground.
- Explain that they are going to discuss what they need to 'bloom' and be the best they themselves can be.

- Ask them what they think they need.
- After each good answer ask a child to come up to the picture and draw a line with a little leaf out to the side to represent the flower growing and write one word that represents the child's answer, somewhere around the flower (below ground or above it).
- Discuss the less obvious things and add to the list including: love, care, rules, goals, guidance, security, safety, experience, friends, encouragement, a home, respect, play, exercise, fairness, education, trust.
- When all the children have contributed, draw a round head for the plant which petals can be attached to.
- Discuss all the things that these help you become – confident, happy, healthy, wise, friendly, kind, respectful, knowing right from wrong, positive, trusting, etc. – and make a list.
- Ask each child to draw and cut out a petal and write on it one of the words from the list.
- Ask the children to bring their petals to the front where they can stick them around the head of the plant, creating a colourful flower.

Variations/extensions

- Using the petals, make a classroom display

Cross-curriculum link

- Science

Share and care

Becoming aware that there are families and children that live in more difficult situations through no fault of their own and that they need our collective help.

Suitable for and curriculum fulfilment

- KS1
- Preparing to play an active role as citizens
- To realise that people and other living things have needs, and that they have responsibilities to meet them

Aims

- To make the class aware that there are children who are in need of help and that their need may be greater than ours
- To understand that we should care that people are in these situations and try to help them
- To understand the idea of giving something of ours to help someone else

Resources

- A charity that accepts what you have chosen to collect and donate:
- http://www.clothesaid.co.uk/
- http://www.redcross.org.uk/Get-involved/Our-shops/Donate-to-our-charity-shops

What to do

- Start by discussing with the class what we need to live and be comfortable.
- Ask the children what would happen if we were unable to have these things and how that could happen.
- Talk about a recent disaster and how these people one day had normal lives and the next everything was turned upside down, in some cases losing all their possessions.

- Ask the children to think about the following:
  - How do you think they feel?
  - Do you think they need help?
  - If we could help them, do you think we should?
- Talk about what a difference it would make for these children, that their need is greater at this moment.
- Discuss how, as a class and a school, we can help.
  There could be a number of different ideas: collecting items in a shoe box, asking parents to help to take clothes to a charity shop, a sponsored walk, run, skipping race.
- Once decided, ask the children to talk in assembly to make their appeal.
- Design and write letters (to be photocopied and sent home) explaining what has been agreed.
- Get pairs of children to collect from each class during the course of the collection week.
- Report back to the school in another assembly about what has happened.
- Find someone from the charity who could come in and pick up any items and money.

Variations/extensions

- Find out if there is someone local who knows or is originally from the region affected who can come in and talk about the area, how it will have been affected, and the help that is needed for things that we might take for granted

Cross-curriculum links

- Geography
- Literacy

Pretend pets

> Asking the children to take care of a pretend pet and to keep a diary of how to look after this pet.

Suitable for and curriculum fulfilment

- KS1
- Preparing to play an active role as citizens
- To realise that people and other living things have needs, and that they have responsibilities to meet them

Aim

- To give children the opportunity to think about how to look after a pet and the responsibilities that this involves

Resource

- Images of typical pets: cats, dogs, rabbits, hamsters, goldfish (have enough of each pet so that a child can choose which one they want)

What to do

- Explain to the class that all pets need looking after every day.
- Ask the children if they have any pets and what they need to do to look after their pets.
- Ask the children to choose a pretend pet, from the selection of images.
- Ask them to research all the things they would need to do to look after their selected pet.
- Give each child a small diary (these can be made by cutting A4 in half and stapling together). This diary is a 7-day diary.
- Ask what the children need to do every day to keep their animal healthy, safe and happy.

- Get the children to write this or draw in their diary. Some of the care activities should be:
  - What does your pet eat?
  - How much time do you need to spend looking after it?
  - Where does it sleep and how does it stay safe?
  - Who will look after it when you go on holiday?
- After a week ask each child to read from their diary (if a child is not yet reading they can describe their pictures).

Variations/extensions

- If any child has a small pet, perhaps the whole class can look after it for a week in the classroom

Cross-curriculum link

- Science

A twig

This activity is about getting the children to recognise that they belong to groups and to see groups and communities as positive things to be a part of, in this case as a class.

Suitable for and curriculum fulfilment

- KS1
- Preparing to play an active role as citizens
- To know that they belong to various groups and communities, such as family and school

Aims

- To recognise that being part of a class means the children are part of a group
- To recognise that there are benefits to being part of a group

Resources

- A bunch of thin twigs approximately 20 cm long or wooden coffee stirrers
- Scissors
- String

What to do

- Ask the children to bring a thin twig about 15–20 cm in length into school, giving one to those without. Alternatively, thin pieces of wood similar to the disposable coffee stirrers.
- Show the class a twig and ask – Can we break it?
- Wait for their answers and then show the children how easily it can be broken.
- Ask each child to make a mark on their twig (it could just be a coloured dot).
- Ask one child to collect all the twigs.
- Ask another child to help you tie the twigs together around the middle.

- Tell the class that you have all of their twigs together now.
- Talk about the bundle representing the class.
- Can this be broken now? Let some of the children try.
- Why not? Because all the sticks are together.
- What are the benefits of doing things together?

Variations/extensions

- Try this activity with sheets of paper

Cross-curriculum link

- Drama

I am here

To explore and discuss different types of groups and explain to the children that they belong to various groups and communities, such as family and school.

Suitable for and curriculum fulfilment

- KS1
- Preparing to play an active role as citizens
- To know that they belong to various groups and communities, such as family and school

Aims

- To explore the different communities to which we belong
- To appreciate that we all like to do different things
- To understand different beliefs and cultural experiences

Resources

- Whiteboard
- Different coloured card circles

What to do

- Start off by asking the children to draw a picture of themselves on a piece of round card.
- Ask the children to draw on another, different coloured piece of round card all the people that they live with.
- Ask them to draw their class and teacher on another piece of round card.
- Ask if anyone in the class is part of any group like a sport class, scouts, Cubs, Brownies or a ballet class. Draw each of these on separate round cards.

- Ask the children to include any religious groups or church groups they belong to.
- Ask the children to stick the drawing of themselves in the middle of the page and then carefully place the other circles around the outside, touching the main circle.
- Let the children have turns showing their picture and talking about the different groups they belong to.

Variations/extensions

- Link with Barnaby Bear and have a look at all the different groups he has been to or has been part of

Cross-curriculum link

- Humanities

Our everyday bag

An activity that can be used to help encourage action in the form of a personalised recycle bag made by the pupil for their family.

Suitable for and curriculum fulfilment

- KS1
- Preparing to play an active role as citizens
- To know what improves and harms the children's local, natural and built environments and about some of the ways people look after them

Aims

- To look at what creates a pleasant playtime environment
- To make the children feel they are playing their part in the bettering of their environment
- To encourage the children and parents to use recycle bags

Resources

- One wholesale cotton bag for each child (**www.stuartmorris.co.uk**)
- Paints or thick felt-tip pens

What to do

- After talking about the environment, litter, plastic bags and our duties both local and global, give each child a bag to design.
- Discuss what the bag is for and why it is a better solution.
- Encourage the children to design the bag based around the lesson or what it will be used for, e.g.
  - Images of the family shopping
  - Image of a beautiful environment or park

- – A slogan that the class has come up with
- – A happy planet
- – Swimming, playing in the park or on the beach.
- Encourage the children to remind their parents to use the bag when they go shopping.

Variations/extensions

- Have a school competition to create a design to be put on a canvas bag that can then be sold to parents to raise money for the school for an environmental project, e.g. planting shrubs, flower boxes, etc. This can be done in conjunction with the school's PTA

Cross-curriculum links

- Humanities
- Art

Park life

A clean, safe and well looked after park can transform a local community. It can be a good meeting place outside school; a place to relax, have fun and get exercise. It is also up to us to respect and look after this valuable resource.

Suitable for and curriculum fulfilment

- KS1
- Preparing to play an active role as citizens
- To know what improves and harms the children's local, natural and built environments and about some of the ways people look after them

Aims

- To recognise the value of our local park in improving our local area/ environment
- To understand the hard work that goes into maintaining it
- To understand that we should use it responsibly

Resource

- A local park warden/keeper

What to do

This activity will be dependent on the type of park that is close to you. Some can be large and green, some are small and concrete.

- Visit your local park.
- While there, discuss what it is used for. What can you do there? Who is using it? Do you like it? Is it tidy?
- Ask a park keeper to come in and speak about the park, including:
  - How it is maintained
  - What problems they deal with

- Who uses the park
- What animals live in the park
- The history of the park
- What we can do to help look after it
- Who is responsible for improvements and investments.

Variations/extensions

- If the park is quite run down you could consider creating an action group to petition the local council to improve the park

Cross-curriculum link

- Geography

Plastic fantastic?

Plastic is everywhere and it is almost impossible to imagine our lives without it, but what is the cost to the environment, both local and global, especially the plastic we use just once before we throw it away?

Suitable for and curriculum fulfilment

- KS1
- Preparing to play an active role as citizens
- To know what improves and harms the children's local, natural and built environments and about some of the ways people look after them

Aims

- To think about plastic and the environmental cost
- To see the bigger picture of what damage plastic can do
- To talk about what we can do to prevent this damage

Resources

- Plastic bottle, toy packaging, disposable bags, plastic rings to hold cans, etc.
- Image of a banana packaged in a plastic tray, sourced from the web
- Web links to plastic facts:
  - Plastic bag use counter USA (top left-hand corner shows a fast-moving counter)
    http://www.container-recycling.org/facts/plastic/

What to do

- Gather the class in a circle.
- Talk to the class about plastic and how we use it every day.
- Talk about the plastic items we use just once and throw away (pass the items around and lay them out in front of everyone).
- What's good about having these things, and how do they help us?

- Make a list.
- Discuss with the class what happens to all this plastic once we have used it.
- Ask the children if they know of any other bad things that are caused by so many plastic disposables.
- Discuss how much plastic we use.
- Show the class the counter to see how quickly bags are used and disposed of.
  - Can they imagine how many that is and how much damage can be done?
- Show the packaged banana image and ask the children what is wrong about it. Vote on whether the pros outweigh the cons.
- Discuss what we can do to reduce the amount of disposable plastic.

Variations/extensions

- Watch the movie *Wall-e*

Cross-curriculum link

- Humanities

What's this from?

A fun and tactile way to get children to look at our household waste differently and to introduce the importance of recycling.

Suitable for and curriculum fulfilment

- KS1
- Preparing to play an active role as citizens
- To know what improves and harms the children's local, natural and built environments and about some of the ways people look after them

Aims

- To recognise and name different domestic waste materials
- To understand that our rubbish comes from many different sources
- To understand that some of these can be recycled and the importance of this

Resources

- An opaque bag for children to pick things out of filled with small example pieces of rubbish we throw away: plastic bottle, toy packaging, glass, paper, wax carton, cellophane food wrap, wood, egg carton, magazine paper, etc.
- Examples of the complete objects they come from to be displayed
- Recycle website:
  http://www.recyclezone.org.uk/

What to do

- Sit in a circle with the objects of rubbish displayed, e.g. plastic bottle, cartons and newspaper.
- Ask a child to pull a piece out of the bag.
- Tell the child to examine it and pass it around the circle.
- Ask what material it is.
- Ask which object it comes from or is used to make and what the object is used for.

- Ask if they know any other things that use this material. Where do they find it, buy it from?
- Repeat for all the objects.
- Ask the children what all these objects have in common (they are things we use and throw away).
- Consider how much rubbish their family, road, school, town, country produce. Ask and talk about where it goes and how we get rid of it.
- Introduce the recycling option.
- Ask the children to guess and separate the objects into recyclable and non-recyclable piles.
- Compare the piles and discuss.
- Ask if they think everything should be recycled and discuss what would be the benefits.
- Show the signs for recycling and why it is important we all do our bit to separate rubbish at home so that we have fewer rubbish dumps.
- Talk about what we can do to have less waste to recycle in the first place. Glass bottles, cloth shopping bags, reuse existing ones.

Variations/extensions

- Here is a website with a list of 10 good recycling websites for children, with activities and information that are easy to digest: http://www.more4kids.info/704/top-10-recycling-websites-for-kids/

Cross-curriculum link

- Humanities

In it together

This activity is about meeting non-teaching staff, understanding what a huge amount goes into running a school and how they are a part of it and have responsibilities.

Suitable for and curriculum fulfilment

- KS1
- Preparing to play an active role as citizens
- To contribute to the life of the class and school

Aims

- To make the children aware of all the things that go on 'in the background' to make the school run properly for their benefit
- To show the 'team effort' that goes into the school
- To ensure that the children understand that they too have responsibilities as part of the school

Resource

- Staff willing to talk for 1–2 minutes about what they do, to answer some simple questions and to say what would or would not happen if they didn't do their job

What to do

- Ask the children if they know what jobs need to be done for them so that they can have a school.
- Tell the children they are going to go for a walk around the school to investigate and talk to people.
- Think of some simple questions they can ask, e.g. What do you do? What would happen if you didn't do your job? What time do you start work? Is what you do hard or easy? What can we do to make your job easier?

- Take the children on a tour of the school to meet as varied a selection of the non-teaching staff as possible.
- Encourage the children to ask as many questions as they like.
- Back in the classroom recap the different jobs.
- Explain that we all have our part to play to make the school a success. What can we do to make our school successful? Can the children remember what the staff said? What else can each of us do to help?
- A successful school is a happy school is a more fun place to be.

Variations/extensions

- Create a set of school rules, not just classroom rules
- Link in with PSHE Developing Good relations 4a: To recognise how their behaviour affects other people

Cross-curriculum link

- Literacy

Kindness chain

This activity is about building a sense of awareness of the importance of contributing positively to the unity of the class and school through acts of kindness. Each child's act of kindness is written on a paper link that will eventually form a paper chain around the whole classroom.

Suitable for and curriculum fulfilment

- KS1
- Preparing to play an active role as citizens
- To contribute to the life of the class and school

Aims

- To understand how contributing to school life through acts of kindness makes them and the school a happier and more harmonious place to be
- To make children feel positive about contributing to school life in this way

Resource

- People-shaped paper chain links that can be stapled together at the hands – lots of them

What to do

- At the beginning of the week, in morning circle time, talk to the children about good deeds, helpfulness and acts of kindness.
- Talk about how these create a more friendly, happier and nicer place to be.
- Tell the children that they are going to create a chain of kindness based upon all the 'good deeds' they have done.
- Explain that for every good deed a link will be created, and these will be joined to form a chain that will work its way round the walls of the classroom so that it will eventually create a full circle.

- Ask the children to remember their acts of kindness throughout the week.
- Explain to them that on Friday they will need to write down each good deed on a paper link.
- On Friday, ask the children to write each of their good deeds on a paper link. Ask each table to join their links and bring them to the front of the class to be linked on the classroom wall.
- Continue this activity every week until the chain has formed a complete circle of kindness around the classroom.

Variations/extensions

- Get each class in the school to participate and to join their paper links together (in school assembly) around the assembly hall

Cross-curriculum links

- Literacy
- Maths

Mucking in

This activity is about taking an active part in the daily necessities of running a classroom, about the children's individual and collective responsibilities in 'doing their share' of what is required.

Suitable for and curriculum fulfilment

- KS1
- Preparing to play an active role as citizens
- To contribute to the life of the class and school

Aims

- To make the children aware of what it takes to keep the classroom/school tidy and how everybody's actions can affect this
- To ensure that the children understand that they too have responsibilities as part of the class/school

Resources

- None needed

What to do

- Explain that as a class we are all responsible for the classroom.
- Explain how we all share the space and we are all responsible for it.
- Introduce a simple class roster for different jobs that need doing.
- Each task should be done in pairs.
- Ask the children to be vigilant to things that may be damaged, missing or broken.
- When the rota changes ask the class to say a collective 'thank you' and give a big clap to the children who have just completed their turn.

Variations/extensions

- Ask and discuss with the children who have completed their turn (at each rota change) what it was like doing the job, how they feel now that they have done it (e.g. proud, responsible) and if there is any advice to pass on to the next children

Cross-curriculum link

- Maths

Playground pals and the friendship bench

Contributing to the life of the school can also be about upholding and nurturing an attitude of care and friendliness in the school. The idea is to have a special place in the playground where children can go if they have no one to play with, which is monitored by children selected to become their playground pals for that playtime. This activity will work better with Year 2 children befriending Year 1 children.

Suitable for and curriculum fulfilment

- KS1
- Preparing to play an active role as citizens
- To contribute to the life of the class and school

Aims

- To show children how looking after each other is an important part of a good and happy school
- To understand that we all have to contribute and participate by taking a shared responsibility

Resource

- A bench or seating area, preferably brightly painted with the name on it, e.g. the Friendship Bench

What to do

Have an assembly that introduces the friendship bench and playground pals (which is best done at the start of the year), explaining what it is about, why the school has it and what to do if you have no one to play with.

In Year 2 classes:

- Talk to Year 2 classes about the life of the school and what it takes to keep the school happy and a fun place to be.
- Talk about responsibilities and setting examples to the younger children, playing their part in keeping the school a happy, considerate and fun place to be.
- Talk about playground pals and what their duties will be:
  - To keep an eye out for children that go to the bench.
  - Introduce themselves.
  - Ask the child's name if they do not know it.
  - Work together to find a game that they can all play together.
- If this idea has been in place for a year or more, explain that last year it was the responsibility of Year 2 to be playground pals and this year it will be theirs.
- Ask and talk about how the last Year 2 did. If there is negative feedback, discuss how they felt when no one came up. Ask if they would like other people to feel that way and talk about how they can do better this year.

In Year 1 classes:

- Explain to the children that if they have nobody to play with they can go to the friendship bench to find someone to play with. If there is nobody there they should sit down and wait for someone to come over and play with them.
- Explain that if they see someone on the bench they can also go over and ask if they want to join in.

Have a daily rota with two playground pals on each day.
Ask the playground pals on duty to report to a named teacher taking playground duty who will be expecting them.
This teacher will remind them of their duty for the playtime.
Have the teacher monitor the bench and keep in contact with the children on duty.
Make special mention of them in class circle time or assembly.

Variations/extensions

- This can be developed into other areas of school life, to team up children who are normally shy with more outgoing children

Cross-curriculum link

- Literacy

Higher or lower?

This is a fun way to get children to understand that money can be used for different things and that these cost different amounts.

Suitable for and curriculum fulfilment

- KS1
- Preparing to play an active role as citizens
- To realise that money comes from different sources and can be used for different purposes

Aim

- To introduce the idea that different things cost different amounts

Resources

- Printed images to represent different ideas and objects, e.g. a holiday, a cinema ticket, a chicken, a loaf of bread, a birthday card, a car, a house, a toy, a packet of sweets
- Two pieces of card with 'A lot' and 'A little' written on them
- Some string
- Two chairs
- Some pegs or sticky tape to attach the pictures to the string

What to do

- At the front of the class place two chairs as far apart as possible.
- Stick the two cards with 'A lot' and 'A little' on each chair.
- Tie or stick the string between the chairs quite firmly.
- Choose a picture and ask the children where on a sliding scale of value the object should go on the string.
- Stand in the middle of the string and ask if it should be 'higher' or 'lower'.

- Stick the picture on the string and starting from that point with another picture ask if the object is valued 'higher' or 'lower' (or 'more' or 'less').
- Move along the line asking, for example, 'even higher?' if they think it is more until you have reached the place they are happy with.
- Discuss as the game goes on and involve the children in expressing their views.
- When the images are all placed, ask them if they wish to rearrange any and discuss.

Variations/extensions

- Using the whiteboard, discuss bigger objects, for example a house or a car – which costs more?

Cross-curriculum link

- Maths

Money!

> Introducing coins, their shape, colour and how they feel is one of the most important starting points in understanding money and its uses.

Suitable for and curriculum fulfilment

- KS1
- Preparing to play an active role as citizens
- To realise that money comes from different sources and can be used for different purposes

Aim

- To introduce coins and their respective values and learn how to recognise them at a glance

Resources

- Realistic toy coins (and bank notes if you wish), one of each sample for each table
- Scissors
- Card
- Grey/silver, brown/bronze and yellow/gold colouring pens
- Paper plates (one for each child)
- Individual images of the outline of the coin shapes and bank notes coloured in (in correct proportion to each other) with grey, brown and yellow for whiteboard

What to do

- Ask the children to trace the outlines of the coins by drawing around them and then colour in each shape with the correct colour (e.g. yellow, brown, grey/silver) and write the correct number value as well as the words that appear on the coins (five pence, one pound).

- Ask the children to cut out the coins and lay them in the correct order of value, lowest to highest.
- Have a guessing game where you show on the whiteboard prepared coins. Point and ask them to work out what the value is just by shape, size and colour. (See Bespoke resource below.)
- Talk about and list on the whiteboard all the things the children can think of that families use money to buy, e.g. food, treats, presents, housing, clothes, TV, car/transport, cinema, clubs they are a member of, etc.
- Ask the children to draw a special design on their plate of a coin for their family.
- Ask the children to write down on their plate all the things from the list that their families use money to buy.

Variations/extensions

- At circle time, mix real coins from different countries with real coins from the UK
  - Ask the children to pick out the UK coins and say what value they are
  - Do the same with bank notes
  - What are the other coins?
  - Explain that different countries have their own money
  - Explain that 1 unit of our money is not necessarily worth 1 unit of the others

Cross-curriculum link

- Maths

Bespoke resource

- See worksheet in Bespoke resources chapter at the end of the book

KS2
Ideas

School uniforms

This activity is about researching, discussing and debating whether your school should have a school uniform, or if your school already has a uniform whether it should be kept or changed.

Suitable for and curriculum fulfilment

- KS2
- Preparing to play an active role as citizens
- To research, discuss and debate topical issues, problems and events

Aims

- To be able to look at all the evidence
- To be able to discuss and debate their views

Resources

- Whiteboard
- Notebooks
- www.bbc.co.uk/learningzone/clips/uniform-vs-non-uniform/6874.html

What to do

- Ask the children for their views on school uniforms.
- What is a uniform? (A uniform is everyone wearing the same; it could be jeans and a white T-shirt.)
- Discuss the advantages and disadvantages of wearing a uniform.
- Write these up under two headings, for and against.
- Research and find out what other children from the school think of school uniforms.
- Give the children a clipboard (or a pad) and get them in the break time to ask other children whether they are for or against school uniform (this could be a simple tick in a 'for' or 'against' column or broken down into years and into gender).

- Ask them to design the form on which they need to record the data.
- Get the children to record their findings.
- Get them to draw a bar graph using the information.
- Ask them to report back findings to the rest of the class.
- Discuss whether anyone changed their mind from their initial views.

Variations/extensions

- Should mobile phones be allowed in schools?

Cross-curriculum links

- Maths
- Literacy

Screen time

This activity asks how much screen time is reasonable. Children should be aware that screen time includes any computer time or television time. It then expands the debate to think about pre-school children and whether they should be allowed screen time.

Suitable for and curriculum fulfilment

- KS2
- Preparing to play an active role as citizens
- To research, discuss and debate topical issues, problems and events

Aims

- To be able to look at all the evidence
- To be able to discuss and debate their views

Resources

- Whiteboard
- Notebooks
- http://news.bbc.co.uk/2/hi/health/8078763.stm

What to do

- Ask the children to sit on the mat.
- Explain to the children what we mean by screen time: TV, computers, PlayStation, Xbox, etc.
- Then ask the children to split the week up and then the weekend.
- Ask them to think about how much screen time they are allowed in the week.
- Is it sometimes necessary to have screen time?
  - For example, computer for doing their homework.

- Then think about the weekend. Should they be allowed more screen time?
- What other things do the children think they should be doing?
- Give the children a chance to discuss their views out loud.
- Then move the topic on to pre-school children. Should they be allowed to watch TV?
- Using the computer, go to the following website:
  http://news.bbc.co.uk/2/hi/health/8078763.stm
  Read this article together and also the recommendations.
- Split the class into two.
- Ask half the class to write a debate about the advantages for pre-school children watching TV.
- Ask the other half to write a debate against pre-school children watching TV.
- Ask the children to swap groups and to read each other's arguments.

Variations/extensions

- To research this argument for primary school children and then for senior school children and finally adults

Cross-curriculum links

- IT
- Literacy

My rights

To look at the UN Convention on the Rights of the Child and to understand why some of the rules were written.

Suitable for and curriculum fulfilment

- KS2
- Preparing to play an active role as citizens
- To know why and how rules and laws are made and enforced, why different rules are needed in different situations and how to take part in making and changing rules

Aims

- To understand why we need rules to protect us
- To think about and discuss why the rules are needed in different situations

Resources

- Internet access on a whiteboard:
  http://www.unicef.org.uk
- Children's Rights page:
  http://www.unicef.org.uk/UNICEFs-Work/Our-mission/Childrens-rights/
- Children's stories:
  http://www.unicef.org.uk/Latest/Photo-stories/Aklimas-Story/
  http://www.unicef.org.uk/Latest/Photo-stories/Carolines-Story/
  http://www.unicef.org.uk/Latest/Photo-stories/Put-it-Right-Charless-Story
  http://www.unicef.org.uk/Latest/Photo-stories/Shumons-Story/
- The 45 articles of UN rights for children:
  http://www.unicef.org.uk/UNICEFs-Work/Our-mission/UN-Convention/
  (On the right under 'Related Documents' is the 'Summary of the Convention on the Rights of the Child')

What to do

- Talk about rules and laws. What are they there for?
- Talk about safety, fairness and respect.
- Talk about different laws for different situations and people; children compared with adults.
- Read the stories of the different children.
- Talk about their lives and discuss what rules could be made to protect these children (using the education, childhood, fairness, voice options on the left of the Children's Rights page).
- Write a list of rules that the class feels would help these children.
- Discuss any more rules that they think would help children in general.
- Talk about how a group of countries from around the world have written some rules to protect children based on what a child needs to survive, grow, participate and fulfil their potential (the United Nations).
- Talk about how some countries have agreed to abide by these rules and others have not.
- Show them a copy of the rights for children and briefly outline the main points.

Variations/extensions

- Look through the 45 articles and see which ones are important and applicable to the lives of the children and discuss. On a map ask the children to find out the countries not signed up to UN rights for children. Why do they think they haven't?
- Raise money for UNICEF:
  http://www.unicef.org.uk/Fundraise/In-emergencies/

Cross-curriculum links

- Geography
- Literacy

You be the judge

This is a very informative interactive website that lets you see the environment of different courts, explains the processes and allows you to pass your judgment on an accused after hearing the evidence for four crimes. It then compares it with the actual sentence.

(It is highly recommended that you go through the website and become familiar with it as one or two strong words are used.)

Suitable for and curriculum fulfilment

- KS2
- Preparing to play an active role as citizens
- To know why and how rules and laws are made and enforced, why different rules are needed in different situations and how to take part in making and changing rules

Aim

- To introduce the Criminal Justice System and how it upholds the law and the processes involved in applying and enforcing it

Resources

- You be the Judge:
  http://ybtj.cjsonline.gov.uk/
- Why sentences are imposed:
  http://sentencing.cjsonline.gov.uk/?id=2&id2=20#a
- A web page that allows you to see crime in the UK in bar chart form and can be broken down in all sorts of ways:
  http://sentencing.cjsonline.gov.uk/?id=2&id2=19

What to do

- Talk about rules and how we have a series of rules called Criminal Law to protect us.
- If someone breaks these laws they have committed a Criminal Offence.
- It is then a matter for the police to investigate and catch the perpetrator.
- When they are caught by the police there is a process that decides whether they are in fact the person who committed the crime, how serious the crime was and what punishment they should get.
- Show the class the website and work through it together.

Variations/extensions

- Have a mock courtroom, with the children taking the different roles, from a judge, to the jury, to the barrister

Cross-curriculum link

- IT

Parallel world

> Being able to act out and explore how anti-social behaviour affects everyone.

Suitable for and curriculum fulfilment

- KS2
- Preparing to play an active role as citizens
- To realise the consequences of anti-social and aggressive behaviours, such as bullying and racism, on individuals and communities

Aim

- To understand what anti-social behaviour (ASB) is and how it affects lives and environments

Resource

- http://www.direct.gov.uk/en/CrimeJusticeAndTheLaw/CrimePrevention/ DG_4001652

What to do

- Discuss anti-social behaviour and the sort of behaviour it incorporates.
- Ask the children to choose or focus on one daily routine (going to the shops, the journey to school, going to the park, playtime in school, etc.) and think how different it would be if the world were anti-social.
- Ask each group to create a short play based around this.
- After each performance explore it further, expanding where necessary.
- Discuss the victim's feelings.
- Would it make you scared to see this?
- How would it affect your routine?
- How would it affect a community?

Variations/extensions

- Ask the children to draw a picture of someone who has been affected by anti-social behaviour and to write words around them that explain their feelings. Ask some of the children to talk about their drawings

Cross-curriculum links

- Drama
- Literacy

The view from the beat

Invite your area's Local Community Police Officer or PCSO (Police Community Support Officer) to give a general overview of anti-social behaviour and its cost to the community as seen through the eyes of someone who deals with it every day and whose job it is to try to stop it.

Suitable for and curriculum fulfilment

- KS2
- Preparing to play an active role as citizens
- To realise the consequences of anti-social and aggressive behaviours, such as bullying and racism, on individuals and communities

Aims

- To understand what constitutes anti-social behaviour
- To understand how it affects individuals
- To understand how it affects the wider community and environment

Resources

If you wish to use these clips in the lesson please look through them and make sure you feel comfortable with all the information, tone of voice and imagery on them and the possible questions or issues they could bring up. Also think about whether the links are suitable for the maturity of the class as a whole.

- Short video by HMIC with comments from people who suffer from ASB:
  http://www.youtube.com/watch?v=_0ADc-r4ub0
- Other reference material:
  http://www.problemneighbours.co.uk/anti-social-behaviour-and-children.html

What to do

- Ask your Local Community Police Officer and/or PCSO (Police Community Support Officer) to come in and talk about anti-social behaviour and crime.
- Ask them to talk about:
  - What is anti-social behaviour?
  - Their job and what it entails to deal with ASB and their views on it.
  - How it can affect the victims.
  - How it changes the lives and habits/routines of the victims.
  - How ASB can affect the community in general, both socially and environmentally.
  - How it makes them feel dealing with it on a daily basis.
- After they have left, discuss what they have said and recap on what constitutes ASB.

Variations/extensions

- The broken window theory (see video for reference): http://www.bbc.co.uk/truthaboutcrime/stories/anti_social_behaviour.shtml)
- Talk about the domino effect that, if we allow small acts of ASB to continue that may not affect us directly, it can change the area we live in on a much greater basis than we realise and eventually it can affect everyone who lives in it including us (we all want to live in a clean, safe and friendly area, etc.)

Cross-curriculum links

- Literacy
- IT

Voices of anti-social behaviour

This activity can be integrated into a discussion about anti-social behaviour and bullying and is based around hearing and reading some of the stories and feelings of people who have been victims.

Suitable for and curriculum fulfilment

- KS2
- Preparing to play an active role as citizens
- To realise the consequences of anti-social and aggressive behaviours, such as bullying and racism, on individuals and communities

Aim

- To gain an understanding of how victims of anti-social behaviour feel and how it affects their lives

Resources

- Whiteboard
- Stories and quotes from people who have been bullied. Please look thoroughly at all these links and make sure you feel comfortable with all the information and imagery on them and the possible questions or issues they could bring up. Also think about whether the links are suitable for the maturity of the class as a whole.
  http://www.bullywatch.org/victims_stories.html
  http://www.bullying.co.uk/index.php/parents/is-child-bully/how-does-bullying-make-a-child-feel.html

What to do

- Ask the children to read out some of the stories chosen from the above websites.
- Split the class up into groups.
- Give each group some photocopies of the stories.

- Discuss between each group how it must have felt for the victims or targets of ASB.
- Ask the children to highlight or write down the words they used to describe how they felt, e.g. scared, sick, lonely, etc.
- Ask someone from each group to stand up and tell the class about the person they have read about, what happened to them and how they felt.
- Ask each group to read out the words they highlighted to describe how the victims felt and write these on the whiteboard.
- Discuss these words and how it makes them feel to hear these stories.

Variations|extensions

- These audio files can be used as a talking point as well for older KS2 children. They are monologues of victim's poems and stories (Bryony and Nick):
http://www.bbc.co.uk/leicester/content/articles/2008/11/12/anti_bullying_monologues_feature.shtml

Cross-curriculum link

- Literacy

Having to choose

This activity focuses on the conflicts that can occur. There are not always simple answers to these problems but they do encourage debate.

Suitable for and curriculum fulfilment

- KS2
- Preparing to play an active role as citizens
- To understand that there are different kinds of responsibilities, rights and duties at home, school and in their community and that these can sometimes conflict with each other

Aim

- To feel comfortable enough with the concepts of responsibilities, rights and duties to be able to apply them to different situations

Resource

- Whiteboard

What to do

- Talk about responsibilities, rights and duties (see 'Places and actions' in this chapter).
- Go through some dilemmas, for example:
  - Saturday school football match vs going to visit your grandmother
  - Best friend's birthday party vs cousin's birthday party
  - Religious festival vs going to school
  - Evening school band concert vs going round to your friend's house to play
  - Going to school vs staying at home and looking after your younger brother/sister as your parent has to go out
  - Playing on your games console vs going to church

- School homework vs Cubs night
- Tidying your room vs down time
- Helping at your brother's birthday party vs going to the park with your friends
- School overnight trip vs helping family at home
- Sleepover vs homework
- Discuss which category each side of the dilemma falls into, i.e. responsibility, right or duty.
- Discuss and debate what the choice should be.
  This can be done by dividing the children into groups and asking a representative of each group to get up and tell the other groups their choice. Alternatively it can be done as an informal, open discussion.
- Encourage the children to talk about their own experiences, what decision they made and why.

Variations/extensions

- Play the game 'know your rights' on the following website: **www.uncrcletsgetitright.co.uk**

Cross-curriculum link

- Literacy

Places and actions

This activity is about getting children to understand and think about the responsibilities, rights and duties they have at home, school and in the community.

Suitable for and curriculum fulfilment

- KS2
- Preparing to play an active role as citizens
- To understand that there are different kinds of responsibilities, rights and duties at home, school and in their community and that these can sometimes conflict with each other

Aims

- To create awareness that we all have responsibilities, duties and rights
- To understand the differences between them
- To consider how these apply to the main areas of their lives

Resource

- Whiteboard

What to do

- Discuss the differences between rights, duties and responsibilities.
  - A right is something that you should expect, e.g. a safe home environment.
  - A duty could be considered a specific act, e.g. tidy your bedroom once a week.
  - A responsibility is more of a moral concept for behaviour, e.g. respect the things around you.

- Discuss with the children the rights, duties and responsibilities that they have at home, at school and within their various communities.
- On paper, under the three headings of Home, School and Community, ask each child to write three or more examples of their rights, responsibilities and duties.
- Gather the answers and write them into a Venn diagram on the whiteboard (the three circles being Home, School and Community).
- Discuss the findings with the children to see the areas that are different and common.

Variations/extensions

- To make individual Venn diagrams

Cross-curriculum link

- Maths

The important things in life

This activity is designed to get the children to think about their relationship with family and friends.

Suitable for and curriculum fulfilment

- KS2
- Preparing to play an active role as citizens
- To reflect on spiritual, moral, social and cultural issues, using imagination to understand other people's experiences

Aims

- To get the children to think about the kind of person they want to be and how they want to be seen by others around them
- To show them they have a choice to see life in a more positive way and that this in itself changes the way the world sees you

Resource

- The important things in life:
  http://academictips.org/blogs/moral-tale-the-important-things-in-life/
  (You may wish to edit the second to last paragraph slightly to suit this age group, e.g. 'Spend time with your family and friends. Take time to talk with your parents. Take time to help and share in the same way your family and friends help and share with you. There will always be time to play games on the computer or watch TV.')

What to do

- Read this story and discuss its meaning with the class.
- Ask the children to make a list of the people who are most important to them.

- Ask the children to make a list of the things that make them and their friends happy, things they can do more of that bring joy and happiness into their lives and the lives of others.

Variations/extensions

- Be someone else! For example, what makes your teacher happy?

Cross-curriculum link

- Literacy

The window

This short, thought-provoking story asks the children to think about its universal meaning regarding our attitude to life and others.

Suitable for and curriculum fulfilment

- KS2
- Preparing to play an active role as citizens
- To reflect on spiritual, moral, social and cultural issues, using imagination to understand other people's experiences

Aim

- To begin to think about and reflect on how we wish to approach life

Resource

- The Window (second story down – needs to be adapted to suit the class): http://www.indianchild.com/inspiring_stories.htm

What to do

- Ask the children either as a class or in groups to read the story and discuss its meaning.
- Talk about the two different people and their different attitudes but concentrate more on the man who described the non-existent view.
- Discuss his attitude to life. There are many things to take from this, but here are a few directions in which to take the discussion:
  - The moral is that a lot of our life is determined by how we choose to look at it, how we choose to live it and how much effort and imagination we are willing to put in.
  - Looking to be positive and happy in life is a matter of choice ... it doesn't just happen to us. We should strive to have a positive outlook that we apply to our daily lives.
  - Our situation is just a small part of what makes us happy.

Variations/extensions

- Another story that is very thought-provoking is this one:
  Don't hope, decide.
  This story is about relationships and takes the example of marriage. This can be easily edited to be just about friends or family. The moral is that a lot of our life is determined by how we choose to look at it and how much effort we are willing to put in
- Hidden gems for thought-provoking discussion can also be found in Aesop's fables, the Jataka Buddhist fables or the Ancient Indian Panchatantra fables which are all easily accessible on the internet. The Jataka fables have been turned into animations that can be viewed on YouTube

Cross-curriculum link

- Literacy

Riddle solving

Ask the children to solve this famous riddle, finding out how differences have been resolved and how there are alternatives by looking at it from a different angle.

Suitable for and curriculum fulfilment

- KS2
- Preparing to play an active role as citizens
- To resolve differences by looking at alternatives, making decisions and explaining choices

Aims

- For children to see situations in a different way and to be able to realise all the alternatives and to realise that there are choices
- To show them compromise involves conceding or sharing but this can still mean you get more than you would have got

Resources

- Whiteboard
- Two bowls with some soft fruit like chopped-up melon
- Two spoons taped to long sticks less than the width of the table

What to do

- Ask the children to sit on the mat.
- Ask them to solve this famous riddle.
- Tell them this scenario:
  - There are two rooms, both of which are identical.
  - In each room there is a table and 12 chairs, 6 either side facing each other.
  - In each of the chairs sits a person (in total 12 people).

- On the table are 12 bowls filled with food in front of each of them.
- Beside each bowl is a very long-handled spoon (about the width of the table) and so long they cannot put their spoon into their own mouth.
- There are only two rules that they must all abide by:
  - No one is allowed out of his or her chair.
  - You can only eat the food using the spoons (not with your hands or putting your head in the bowl).
- In one of the rooms the 12 people are hungry and miserable, as they cannot get their spoons into their own mouths.
- In the other room the 12 people are eating away merrily and all having a great time.
  How can this be?
  Ask two children to sit either side of the table with a bowl and a spoon in front of each of them and discuss the riddle with the class.
- The answer is, of course, they feed each other. At this point the two children should have a go at feeding each other the soft fruit. Discuss.
  Compromise, working together, thinking less selfishly are the keys to resolving differences.

Variations/extensions

- In PE, try relay races, where children have to practise passing the baton

Cross-curriculum links

- Literacy
- PE

Two ways

To take two different scenarios and the children role-play looking at the different outcomes.

Suitable for and curriculum fulfilment

- KS2
- Preparing to play an active role as citizens
- To resolve differences by looking at alternatives, making decisions and explaining choices

Aim

- To consider the concept of compromise and choices

Resource

- Two exercises on the whiteboard showing two very different scenarios

What to do

- Ask the children if they have ever been in a situation where they have had to compromise but they were still happy with the outcome.
- Write up these scenarios on the whiteboard:
  - Bedtime: your parent says it's time for bed but you want to watch a programme on TV.
  - Film: at the local multi-screen cinema one of you wants to see an action movie while the other wants to see a comedy.
  A more ambiguous one:
  - Drink: you are with a friend and you are both thirsty. Both of you have 45p. You both want different drinks that cost 60p each.
- The children then work in pairs and role-play each side (choosing examples from the board) working out how to solve the problem.

- Choose several pairs of children to re-enact their role-play in front of the class.
- Ask the children to discuss the different points of view and look for possible compromises if none was reached, e.g.
  - Bedtime: record the programme and watch it the next day.
  - Film: see which film is on next week and go to watch that one next week. See what other films are on.
  - Drink: pool their money or have no drink. Both need to put in 30p each, but if one puts in more does that person get to choose?

Variations/extensions

- Ask the children to think of their own scenarios working in pairs

Cross-curriculum links

- Drama
- Literacy

Democracy foundations/building blocks

Although democracy is a form of political organisation that is founded on the idea of equal control, it has also required many underlying and interconnected beliefs that are now considered inseparable from it. This activity aims to highlight the theoretical building blocks and principles that underpin what is now seen as the basis for a democracy.

Suitable for and curriculum fulfilment

- KS2
- Preparing to play an active role as citizens
- To know what democracy is, and about the basic institutions that support it locally and nationally

Aims

- To understand what democracy means
- To understand the principles that underlie modern democracy
- To understand what it means for us, our responsibilities and what our expectations should be

Resources

- http://en.wikipedia.org/wiki/Democracy
- http://en.wikipedia.org/wiki/Civil_liberties
- http://en.wikipedia.org/wiki/Human_rights
- Crayons for rubbings
- Thick marker pens
- Whiteboard

What to do

- Ask if anyone knows what democracy is.
- Talk about its origins in Greece.
- Talk about the basic principle of equal power and say, and how the people choose through election how the country should be run.
- Talk about equality and fairness.
- Discuss in what other ways we should be seen as equal and treated the same.
- Write down some of the underlying basic principles (building blocks) that have come to be expected in a democracy in respect to our relationship with the government:
  - Equality, respect, protection, transparency, privacy
  - Freedoms of expression, speech, religion, liberty, security
  - Freedom from torture, slavery, forced labour, prejudice
  - To have dignity, liberty, fair trial and the ability to protest or disagree.
- Talk about life without these.
- Ask the children to draw their own bricks (this can be done as rubbings from brick walls).
- Ask them to write one of the various principles on their brick so that all the principles are covered.
- Build the wall using the bricks.
- Talk about what happens if some of the bricks are taken away, how it becomes destabilised.
- Talk about our responsibilities to maintain these foundations, our respect of these blocks, the upholding of them and the importance to have our say.

Variations/extensions

- Write a short story about the history of democracy

Cross-curriculum links

- Humanities
- Literacy
- Art

Everyone counts

An easy way to show the main principle of democracy in action with the children getting to vote on an issue and seeing it happen.

Suitable for and curriculum fulfilment

- KS2
- Preparing to play an active role as citizens
- To know what democracy is, and about the basic institutions that support it locally and nationally

Aim

- For the children to have a basic idea of democracy and to feel empowered in their decision-making process

Resources

- Whiteboard
- Printed or photocopied paper with the ideas on, with boxes next to them to tick
- Box at front of class with slot
- List of class names to tick off when they have voted
- http://www.parliament.uk/about/mps-and-lords/members/partysystem/
- http://www.parliament.uk/about/how/

What to do

- Ask – What is democracy?
- Explain to the children the basics of the democratic process.
- What institutions support it?
  - From a local level (Councillors)

- To voting for an MP and their party to lead the country in the Houses of Parliament
- Or voting for a representative in the European Parliament in Brussels.
- Explain that on one day everyone in the country votes and where this takes place, e.g. school hall, church, community centres, etc. There is also the possibility of voting through the post if you are unable to visit your designated local voting hall.
- Ask the children how they might all agree on one of the following ideas:
  - What should they do on their last day at school before half-term or the end of term?
  - What theme would they like to have for their end-of-year school party?
  - Where would they like to go for their end-of-school class trip?
- Ask the children to get into groups and come up with one idea, each thinking of some reasoning to back it up bearing in mind they will have to present their idea to the rest of the class.
  - If some of the groups have the same idea they can join together.
  - Each group should then present their idea to the rest of the class.
  - Encourage the children to debate and ask relevant and logistical questions.
- Once they have all spoken, tell them it is time to vote.

Ask one child to sit next to the box and tick off the names of the children when they vote.

The children should then cast their votes by coming to the front of the class, taking a piece of paper, ticking the box they agree with, folding the paper and putting it in the box. (You could create a booth with a sheet across if you want.)

When they have all voted (not forgetting the name ticker) ask three other children to come up and empty the box. Ask two of them to put them into different piles based on the choices and ask the third child to go through all the piles, make sure they are correct and then add up the number in each pile but not to tell the class who has won.

The numbers are written down and passed to the teacher to read out. Whatever the result is, let the class do!

Variations/extensions

- Who decides who is a prefect? Or a monitor? This is a whole school debate; think about how this could be organised

Cross-curriculum link

- Literacy

Classroom parliament

Recreating a parliament in a classroom – with three parties, a topic and a vote.

Suitable for and curriculum fulfilment

- KS2
- Preparing to play an active role as citizens
- To know what democracy is, and about the basic institutions that support it locally and nationally

Aim

- To give an idea of what goes on in Parliament or in their local Council chambers and how these institutions decide, through debate and voting, what should be done

Resources

- http://www.parliament.uk/about/how/role/debate/
- http://www.parliament.uk/about/how/role/traditions/
- http://www.macmillandictionary.com/thesaurus-category/british/In-the-UK-Parliament-and-Assemblies
- Watch it live: http://www.bbc.co.uk/iplayer/tv/bbc_parliament/watchlive
- Watch recorded: http://www.bbc.co.uk/iplayer/tv/bbc_parliament
- Big stickers to colour in with their party colour and name
- Whiteboard

What to do

- Recap about elections and how we vote to choose a party, i.e the party with the greatest number of elected representatives (MPs) winning.
- Explain that you are going to look at what happens in Parliament and how the MPs make the decisions that affect our country in between the elections.

- Show the children a picture of the House of Commons.
- Explain that the class is going to have its own pretend parliament.
- Explain that in this parliament there are three parties: the Orange, the Green and the Purple.
  - Orange won the General Election, Green came second and purple third.
- Split the class into three parties with Orange having the majority. (So out of 30 children maybe 16 are Orange, 9 are Green and 5 are Purple.)
- Explain that they are the MPs that were voted in during the election.
- Ask them to colour in their sticker with their party colour and write their name underneath, 'The Right Honourable ...'
- Divide the room into roughly two halves; get the Orange party to sit on one side and the rest on the other side.
- The teacher is the Speaker of the House and sits on a chair at the end of the line.
- Each party is given a proposal or 'Bill' to discuss in parliament, e.g.
  - We should close all parks and give every child a handheld games console for free.
  - We should pay to use a library.
  - Children should decide what time they go to bed.
  - We shouldn't have lessons in school; we should just play all day.
- A representative of one of the parties stands up and makes their proposal (Bill).
- Write the proposal on the whiteboard.
- Have a debate about it and vote whether it should be approved or not.
- They can agree (aye), disagree (no) or abstain (say nothing and keep their hands down).
- Count up and show the results on the whiteboard.

It is up to you how many technical terms you wish to introduce or feel are appropriate.

Explain that this process takes place in local Councils as well as in Parliament, the House of Lords and in the European Parliament in Brussels.

Variations/extensions

- A trip to the House of Commons or a visit to the local Council chambers to see the whole thing in action

Cross-curriculum link

- Maths

Homeless

Introducing the idea of volunteering by having someone who works within the local community come in and speak to the children about the work that they do, its importance, why they did it in the first place and what motivates them to keep on doing it.

Suitable for and curriculum fulfilment

- KS2
- Preparing to play an active role as citizens
- To recognise the role of voluntary, community and pressure groups

Aims

- To introduce the idea of volunteer work
- To introduce and discuss empathy for people in different situations
- To have the opportunity to volunteer for something and to put into practice what they have learnt by cooking/baking for the homeless
  This idea is not for the faint-hearted: it will be totally dependent on finding the right kind of organisation that can accept the food and will involve a certain amount of logistical organisation

Resources

- A homeless volunteer group/homeless association or church group that can:
  - Send someone to talk to the children about what they do
  - Accept food to hand out to homeless people
  (This will involve some organising with the group)
- Use of the school kitchen to prepare and cook some food
- If possible, someone who is helped by the volunteer group to talk about the difference it makes
- http://www.shelter.org.uk/

What to do

- Find a local homeless volunteer organisation that can send someone in to talk to the children.
- Ask them to talk about what they do, its importance, why they did it in the first place and what motivates them to keep on doing it.
- Ideally, if it is possible, get someone who benefits from the work to come in to talk about the difference the work makes and what it would be like without it.
- Discuss with the class empathy, community and our role/place within that.
- Discuss the ideas behind altruism and donation of time.
- Explain that understanding others' situations is an important part of creating better communities.
- Ask if any of the class would like to donate time to help.
  - This could be bringing in food to prepare, helping with the menu, chopping vegetables (always with adult supervision), or baking at home and bringing in the cakes to donate or to raise money.
- Organise an after-school cooking event – this will need the co-operation of the kitchen staff for peeling and chopping up veg and cooking that can then be sent that day for the evening meal for the homeless kitchen (make sure to take photos).
- One of the teachers to go to the homeless kitchen and take more photos to show the class.
- With the children create a wall with the photos on, recipes for the food, etc.
- Ask the head teacher to tell the school assembly what the children did and to give them a round of applause.

Variations/extensions

- If possible, this could be an annual activity around a family festival (Christmas) that creates thoughtfulness, pride and nurtures good role models for the school

Cross-curriculum link

Other famous volunteers:

- History (Mary Seacole: http://www.maryseacole.com/maryseacole/pages/)

I can help

To get the children involved in raising awareness for a local project in the community by giving up their time.

Suitable for and curriculum fulfilment

- KS2
- Preparing to play an active role as citizens
- To recognise the role of voluntary, community and pressure groups

Aims

- To realise the importance of giving up our time to help with voluntary organisations
- To appreciate the work local community groups and charities do tirelessly

Resources

This activity will take a lot of organisation from the teachers involved

- A local voluntary or community organisation to come in and talk about what they do and make a second visit
- Individual questions on cards for the children to ask (make sure the person coming in has seen these questions and has had time to prepare for them)
- Sponsorship templates
- A letter to parents about the local group along with an explanation of what the class will be doing

What to do

- Discuss with the children the different roles of voluntary organisations and community groups.
- Did they know there any local organisations that help with local issues?

- Tell the children someone is coming in to talk to them, and these are some suggested questions that the children can ask (you can put these on cards to hand out beforehand):
  - Who do you help?
  - What do you do?
  - How often do you do it?
  - How do you change things?
  - Why do you do it?
  - How does it make you feel?
  - Is it easy or hard work?
  - Where does the money come from?
  - What would happen if you didn't do it?
  - What can we do to help?
- Ask the children if they would like to help.
- Suggest a number of sponsored things to do:
  - Sponsored walk, run, skip, etc.
  - Each child can do a separate event (this can be done and adjudicated during PE).
- Ask the children to design a poster/letter to take home.
- Hold the event at school during PE.
- Collect forms and money.
- Hand the money over to the representative of the organisation (preferably the same person who came in to talk).
- Ask the organisation to write a letter to the class telling them what the money has been used for, etc.

Variations/extensions

- If a lot of classes in the school have been involved, write a letter to the local newspaper and if possible invite them to come in and interview the children handing over their donation to the community group

Cross-curriculum links

- Literacy
- IT
- PE

Pressure groups

Introducing the idea of a pressure group, what they do and what part they play in society.

Suitable for and curriculum fulfilment

- KS2
- Preparing to play an active role as citizens
- To recognise the role of voluntary, community and pressure groups

Aims

- To understand that we are not powerless to create change in our community or on a wider scale
- To understand that there are acceptable channels and processes for people who do not hold positions of power to make known their views or protest against bodies that do not have the best interests of their environment and community at heart
- To help the children feel empowered to be heard by people in official positions of influence

Resources

- Different pressure groups in the UK:
  http://en.wikipedia.org/wiki/Pressure_groups_in_the_United_Kingdom

What to do

- Explain that they are often people who feel strongly about something.
- Talk about the different kinds of pressure group, i.e. from large organised groups to small community groups, and the vast range of concerns they have both large and small.
- Talk about how successful they can be.

- Ask if there is anything that the children would like to see change.
  - Talk about a specific concern and what they feel about it, the rights and wrongs, etc.
  - The subject can be as macro or micro as you wish, from something nationally topical to something local within the community or based around the school.
  - Some possible examples are closing down a park, cinema or post office, getting rid of lollipop ladies/men, or people parking outside the school gates. Ideally it should be something that is actually happening.
  - How would they go about creating a pressure group?
- Discuss a name for the group.
  - How do they go about being heard?
  - Who do they contact and how?
  - Create a mini plan of action.
- Design a poster to create awareness and support for your chosen subject.
- Ask the children to compose a letter to a local MP or local Ward Councillor inviting them to come in to talk to them about the problem.

Variations/extensions

- If this is an actual local situation where there is already an action group, does the class agree with this action group?
- Ask the children to write to the local newspaper to invite them to be present when presenting the local MP or Councillor with the open letters they have written
- Look at a case study: http://www.greenpeace.org.uk/
- Martin Luther King: http://www.bbc.co.uk/history/historic_figures/king_martin_luther.shtml

Cross-curriculum links

- Literacy
- IT
- Art and Design

Same but different

To find out what it means to be British and create a calendar of cultural and religious events.

Suitable for and curriculum fulfilment

- KS2
- Preparing to play an active role as citizens
- To appreciate the range of national, regional, religious and ethnic identities in the United Kingdom

Aim

- To celebrate our diversity and our rich cultural references

Resource

- Whiteboard with a world map

What to do

- Discuss with the children what it means for them to be British.
- Ask the children if any of their parents, grandparents or great-grandparents came from anywhere else in the world.
- Identify these places on the map.
- Look at the map and see all the different religions, customs, festivals, languages and food that make up multi-cultural Britain.
- Put together a calendar marking down each of the different festivals, celebrations, holy days, religious days and holidays.

Variations/extensions

- To celebrate in class each of the different festivals that a child in the class celebrates at home
- Ask if a parent can come in and talk about it

Cross-curriculum link

- Literacy

World food

To create a menu from all the different types of restaurants and cuisines found in the UK.

Suitable for and curriculum fulfilment

- KS2
- Preparing to play an active role as citizens
- To appreciate the range of national, regional, religious and ethnic identities in the United Kingdom

Aim

- To celebrate our diversity through food

Resources

- World map
- Different menus or recipes from different types of ethnic food, e.g. English, Scottish, Welsh, Indian, Chinese, Thai, Italian, Caribbean, African, Turkish, Greek, American, etc.

What to do

- Ask the children what their favourite foods are.
- Ask the children to look at and pass the menus around.
- Can they identify, for different types of food, what the origins are?
- Look at the world map and put a pin in the different places.
- Ask the children to think of a World Menu.
- Can they write a menu with different starters, main courses and desserts using all the different regions on the world map.

Variations/extensions

- To use IT to design and type in a menu

Cross-curriculum links

- Literacy
- IT
- Humanities

Finite resources

The children are in charge of a country and have to decide how a resource should be allocated when there is only a finite amount available.

Suitable for and curriculum fulfilment

- KS2
- Preparing to play an active role as citizens
- To understand that resources can be allocated in different ways and these economic choices affect individuals, communities and the sustainability of the environment

Aim

- To understand the dilemma of resource allocation

Resources

- http://www.fao.org/docrep/u8480e/u8480e0c.htm
- http://www.waterfootprint.org/index.php?page=files/InfoGraphics
- Prepared bar chart (see Bespoke resources), one for each child
- Whiteboard

What to do

- Explain that everyone in the class is going to have to be in charge of a country and to decide how a resource is to be allocated (water in this case).
- Explain that they have x number of units (in this case maybe 8) that the country has.
- They have to decide where it is to be used.
- The bar chart can be filled by colouring in the boxes from the bottom of each column up.
- Show an example on the whiteboard, discussing and debating the dilemmas.

- Encourage the children to fill in their own sample.
- Ask some of the children to explain their choices to the class and discuss.

Variations/extensions

- Change the number of units available, the number of uses, the number of column options or the resource, e.g. oil

Cross-curriculum links

- Literacy
- IT
- Maths

Bespoke resource

- See worksheet in Bespoke resources chapter at the end of the book

My future world

The Earth has a finite amount of resources. How many planets we would need to live the way we do and what changes we need to make to live our lives sustainably?

Suitable for and curriculum fulfilment

- KS2
- Preparing to play an active role as citizens
- To understand that resources can be allocated in different ways and these economic choices affect individuals, communities and the sustainability of the environment

Aims

- To gain an awareness and understanding of how our lifestyles are more than likely incompatible with the way we use the Earth's resources at the moment
- To discuss the various practical things that we can do to reduce our use
- To discuss alternative energy sources

Resources

- Whiteboard connected to internet:
  http://www.ecologicalfootprint.com/
- http://my2050.decc.gov.uk/ This is a great website but you will need to play around with it for a while to work out the best way to lead the lesson
- http://www.planet-positive.org/how_2_calculator.php

What to do

First get to know the websites and how changing the various answers changes the results radically. From this you can tailor your lesson.

- Talk about finite resources, especially oil.

- Ask if they know what oil is used for and compile a varied list, e.g. travel, food production and packaging, clothes, heating and lighting and all the things made out of plastic.
- Ask if we have enough oil.
- Talk about how our consumption is exceeding environmental limits.
- Talk about the side-effects of using all this oil, i.e. CO_2 emissions.
- Introduce the websites to the children.
  - Briefly explain that for our planet to survive we need to use only one planet's worth of resources (show them the planets on the website).
- Answer the questions and see how many planets we need to survive.
- Show the class how we have to live to have a sustainable planet by changing the settings.
- Discuss what changes we can start to make.
  - Will it be hard or easy?
  - Do we have a choice?

Variations/extensions

- Talk about the other sources of energy we could use (sunlight, water, etc.) that can replace or cut down on the amount of oil we use

Cross-curriculum link

- IT

News views

News stories are presented in many ways, both with technology and with different emphasis.

Suitable for and curriculum fulfilment

- KS2
- Preparing to play an active role as citizens
- To explore how the media present information

Aims

- To understand that:
    - news is presented and reported in a variety of ways and formats
    - it can contain different information
    - stories can be written with different emphasis on different aspects of the event, e.g. human interest, political or entertainment
    - it is important to read/see/hear a variety of reports to get a fuller picture

Resources

- As varied a selection of national newspapers and magazines as possible that contain the topic
- Internet access (web news, iPlayer for radio and TV news, news clips on the BBC)
- If you have time, recordings of the news on radio and of the news on television (BBC radio or TV player, YouTube)

What to do

- Pick a subject that, ideally, is currently in the news and is being reported extensively on all media platforms (web, magazine, newspaper and TV). It is important that the story is being reported from as many different perspectives as possible (human, political, social, financial, etc.). The Chilean miners rescue would have been a great example with human interest, politics and gossip.

- Ask about and discuss all the different media/platforms used to present the news.
- Ask the children to look for the story chosen and cut out, take notes or print out the articles.
- Discuss the different ways in which the story has been reported:
  - The different facts and how not all of them are in all of the reports
  - Pictures, what they show and why they were chosen
  - Different people that have been interviewed (people involved, witnesses, politicians, officials, etc.)
  - The different ways stories can be categorised: human interest, political, geographical/science, financial, etc.
- Discuss how the above gives a better, all-encompassing image of what is going on.

Variations|extensions

- Points of view: an old *Guardian* newspaper television advert: http://www.youtube.com/watch?v=E3h-T3KQNxU
  This is a good 30-second video to show the class that instantly sparks debate. It is a good analogy for understanding that it is important to see things from as many points of view as possible to understand a situation properly. This can be applied to show that news sometimes does not contain the full story or that it can contain contradictory information. It can also be brought up that different newspapers have different allegiances politically and are used to influence the way we think. We should not take things at face value, and it is important to get as many different views as possible

Cross-curriculum links

- Literacy
- IT

Pictures tell tales

> This activity encourages children to see that the captions that accompany photographs can often shape our opinion of what we see happening.

Suitable for and curriculum fulfilment

- KS2
- Preparing to play an active role as citizens
- To explore how the media present information

Aims

- To understand the importance of captions that accompany photos in telling a story
- To think more carefully about what captions are telling us

Resources

- Magazines of all sorts
- Scissors
- Glue/tape
- Blank paper
- Image: Mugging (an ambiguous image of a man being held by a group of people):
  http://4.bp.blogspot.com/_PxyKc1uIRZc/S2BGW-YK8BI/AAAAAAAAACA/
  D81rhHVZiCk/s1600-h/mugging+cropped.jpg
- Captions:
  - In the past mugging used to be a big problem
  - In the past groups of people used to chase and catch muggers

What to do

- Show the children a photo (like above) along with a caption.
- Ask them what they think the picture is telling them.
- Show them the same picture with another caption that contradicts the first.

- Ask them their opinion now.
- Ask them why they have changed their minds.
- Talk about how words in a caption can change the way we view something.
- Split the class into groups and ask them to work together to choose a picture that they can add two contrasting captions.
- Ask each group to show the class the image with the first caption and then the second.
- Discuss the images and how they change our perceptions.

Variations/extensions

- Image: Homeless people eating:
  e.g. http://daisychaindays.co.uk/blog/wp-content/uploads/2011/02/g1_u68499_homeless.jpg
- Captions:
  - Many homeless people have turned their backs on our society. They become unclean, unhealthy and can spend a lot of time in public places making people feel uncomfortable. They often go hungry and can end up begging for food or money
  - Many unfortunate homeless are extremely grateful for the kindness of people donating time, help and food. For Dave and John, who have no money or home, this food can be the difference between life and death, especially in the long cold winters
- Show them the image with the two captions:
  - Discuss how these captions do not contradict each other but still give a different story
  - Discuss how the first caption plays to our stereotyping of the homeless and is negative
  - Discuss how the second caption is more positive and personalises the situation
  - Discuss stereotyping and prejudice and how words and pictures can subtly form or reinforce our views

Cross-curriculum link

- Literacy

Scoop!

This activity is for older KS2 children. It introduces the kind of information found in newspapers and encourages the analysis of the construction and content of a news article. By the end they should have read an article, understood it and created their own newspaper article based on it.

Suitable for and curriculum fulfilment

- KS2
- Preparing to play an active role as citizens
- To explore how the media present information

Aims

- To read an article, understand it and describe it
- To express personal and group views on topical issues in their local community

Resources

- Ideally, copies of the same edition of your local newspaper, otherwise a few copies of a national newspaper
- Newspaper page layouts with measurements for the story boxes (see Bespoke resources which is based on A3 paper size)
- Rulers
- Different thickness pens
- General art materials

What to do

- Have some copies of the local paper.
- Group the children and ask them to pick out stories of interest and highlight them.

- List the stories from the groups and discuss:
  - Did they pick the same stories?
  - What did they choose and why?
- Discuss a particular story that perhaps they all picked:
  - What is the story about?
  - What facts are there?
  - Are there quotes from people?
  - Is there a picture?
- Discuss how the article is constructed/laid out, i.e. headline, sub-head, copy, pictures and captions.
- Ask and discuss why articles are broken down this way and how they help the reader.
- Tell the class they are going to make their own version of the newspaper they have just been looking at.
- Discuss and agree a handful of stories that should be included and decide which of these is the most important/headline story (can be as many or few as you want).
- Split the class into small groups. Each group will have one or two stories to write and are designated boxes from the template.
- Designate the chosen stories; the rest of the class can choose any story they want from the paper.
- They will have to measure out their box, re-read the story, come up with a new headline, write a summary of the story and, if they want to, draw a picture to go with it, with a caption. They decide how to divide their space.
- Stick the articles over their corresponding places on the template and ask the children to read out their article.

Variations/extensions

- Talk about the different sections of news and what information they contain
- Send 'reporters' to go to various primed people in school (head teacher, school council members, teacher in charge of a school sports team, etc.)
  - Ask questions about what has happened recently; what issues are important at the moment; things that are going to happen (e.g. sports results, who won/scored? Are there any fund-raising events coming up/just gone? How much money was raised? When is the next one? What does the school need? Any class trips recently?)

- Back in the class discuss which of these stories should be included in a school newspaper
- Make a paper to be distributed around the school
- If you have a video camera you can make a news bulletin to show the school in assembly
  - Consider the sets, clothes, filming and editing, as well as the reporting
  - Each class could do a different end-of-term report

Cross-curriculum links

- Literacy
- PSHE 2a
- IT

Bespoke resource

- See example with measurements based on an A3 sheet in Bespoke resources chapter at the end of the book

Chapter 3

Developing a healthy, safer lifestyle

Introduction

Some of the following activities can be used for either KS1 or KS2 but it is really up to the teacher to use their discretion knowing the ability of their class.

There are fourteen areas that need to be covered in KS1 and KS2 in this chapter. All the activities have been laid out following this order and below each title is a full description of which one it relates to.

As the title of the chapter suggests, children are given an awareness of why they need to look after themselves, what to bear in mind and practical ways to help them achieve it. Key Stage 2 also tackles taboo subjects head on, dispelling myths and arming the children with knowledge to empower them to make sound decisions.

Key Stage 1

There are seven areas in Key Stage 1 that need to be covered and by the end of this stage pupils should have a good grounding in them. The seven areas are as follows:

- To understand how to make simple choices that improve their health and well-being
- To know how to maintain personal hygiene
- To understand how some diseases spread and can be controlled
- To understand the process of growing from young to old and how our needs change
- To know the names of the main parts of the body
- To know that all household products, including medicines, can be harmful if not used properly
- To know rules for, and ways of, keeping safe including basic road safety and about people who can help them to stay safe.

Key Stage 2

There are seven areas again here that need to be covered and these broadly consolidate and build upon what they have learnt in KS1. The chapter also expands upon areas that are relevant to the children's burgeoning independence and social interaction. The seven areas are:

- To understand what makes a healthy lifestyle, including the benefits of exercise and healthy eating, what affects mental health and how to make informed choices

- To understand that bacteria and viruses can affect health and that following simple, safe routines can reduce their spread
- To understand how their bodies change as they approach puberty
- To know which commonly available substances and drugs are legal and illegal, their effects and risks
- To be able to recognise the different risks in different situations and then decide how to behave responsibly, including sensible road use, and judging what kind of physical contact is acceptable or unacceptable
- To understand that pressure to behave in an unacceptable or risky way can come from a variety of sources, including people they know, and how to ask for help and use basic techniques for resisting pressure to do wrong
- To know the school rules about health and safety, basic emergency aid procedures and where to get help.

KS1
Ideas

Food race

A race based on the 'fuel' that the children choose to get them to the finishing line. Each food has a number on the back that relates to how much they move forwards (or backwards!).

Suitable for and curriculum fulfilment

- KS1
- Developing a healthy, safer lifestyle
- To understand how to make simple choices that improve their health and well-being

Aims

- To get the children to think about their choice of snacks and how a range of snacks can affect them differently
- To know how to make healthy choices in what they eat

Resources

- Printed images of different food snacks with numbers on the back. The number relates to the healthiness of each snack (can be from –1 to +2)
- Pieces of paper to lay on the floor as markers for each step forward or backwards they take

What to do

- Place the images on the whiteboard.
- Lay 15–20 pieces of paper on the floor to act as 'step' markers. The fifth one should have START on it (this is because some children may end up going backwards) and the final one should have FINISH on it.
- Explain that there is going to be a race. The way to get to the finishing line is to choose the foods they think will get them there first. Each food has a different number on the back that tells them how far they can move. Don't explain that this is about healthy eating.

- Each child chooses one at a time and so the race continues until there is a winner.
- Repeat until you think enough children have understood that different foods have higher or lower values in the game.
- Discuss the race, which foods were the best and the worst, and what conclusions can be drawn.

Cross-curriculum link

- Science

My healthy meal

By getting the children to compare their favourite meal with a healthy meal, this activity aims to help them become proactive in making choices to improve their diet.

Suitable for and curriculum fulfilment

- KS1
- Developing a healthy, safer lifestyle
- To understand how to make simple choices that improve their health and well-being

Aims

- To make the children aware of what makes a healthy, balanced meal
- To get the children to compare their favourite/normal meal with a healthy one
- To encourage the children to think about how to improve their diet

Resources

- Paper plates or worksheet similar to the one shown in Bespoke resources
- Images of the different food types and resource images for healthy eating (depending on age: food pyramid, breakdown of percentages of food groups, etc.)

What to do

- Ask the children to draw and write on their plate either their favourite meal or what they had last night for dinner.
- Ask some to come to the front and tell the class what they have on their plate and encourage them to expand on their descriptions if necessary; for example, if they say pizza, do they know what was on the pizza?

- Talk about a healthy, balanced diet in as much detail as is appropriate to their age.
- Ask the children to 'improve' their meal by adding some things and/or taking away and replacing other parts.
- Ask some children to talk about their meal, what they have changed and why.

Variations/extensions

- Ask the kitchen staff at school if they could follow a menu that the class chooses

Cross-curriculum link

- Science

Bespoke resource

- See worksheet in Bespoke resources chapter at the end of the book

Happy Tummy Cafe menu

This activity is about balanced diets, talking about and then designing a menu, which uses all the different food groups.

Suitable for and curriculum fulfilment

- KS1
- Developing a healthy, safer lifestyle
- To understand how to make simple choices that improve their health and well-being

Aims

- For the children to understand that a balanced diet improves our health and makes us stronger
- To know the difference between healthy food and unhealthy food
- To know how to make healthy options in what they eat

Resources

- Images of different food
- Whiteboard and digital projector (optional)
- Copy of your school menu
- Preparation on tabletops:
  - A4 pages folded in half lengthways with Happy Tummy Cafe written at the top (like a menu)
- Food magazines
- Scissors
- Glue

What to do

- Ask the children to sit on the mat.
- Have prepared different images of food (these can be found from magazines, cards, etc.).

- Ask the children what their favourite food is.
- Ask the children what they might have at home for dinner.
- Look at how these foods can be separated into healthy food and other food that we shouldn't eat too often. (There should be two columns on the whiteboard which separate the healthy and non-healthy food.)
- Talk to the children about what food is for and that healthy food does this so much better than unhealthy food, and that unhealthy food can often do the opposite if too much of it is eaten.
- At this stage you can also talk briefly about the different food types.
- Look at your own school menu and discuss it.
- Ask the children to go back to the table and create their own healthy menus by cutting out and sticking the food images on their menu and writing on the names of the food.
- The children can then prepare their menus individually.
- Finally ask the children back to the mat where they can show and talk about their menus.

Variations/extensions

- Ask the kitchen staff at school if they could follow a menu that the class chooses
- Ask the person who prepares the school menu to come and discuss it with the class and the class could prepare questions

Cross-curriculum link

- Science

Cover that sneeze

Colds can be a big part of the first few weeks of term. This activity teaches children why it is important to cover their mouths and noses properly when they sneeze.

Suitable for and curriculum fulfilment

- KS1
- Developing a healthy, safer lifestyle
- To know how to maintain personal hygiene

Aim

- To teach the children why it is important to cover their mouths and noses when they sneeze by showing them how far germs can spread

Resources

- A long measuring tape or ball of string
- Sheets of tissue paper/toilet paper

What to do

- Explain to the children that sneezing when you have a cold spreads tiny germs – most children sneeze at about 90 mph with as many as 40,000 germs in each sneeze.
- Choose four children.
- Ask one of the children to sit on a chair, one to hold a single sheet of tissue and two to hold a measuring tape.
- Ask the seated child to blow as hard as possible to make the sheet of tissue move.
- Measure the furthest distance.
- Ask some other children to have a go and see if they can do better.
- Sit everyone back at their desks and ask a child to hold the end of the measuring tape/string above their head.

- Walk in a circle around the child with the string extended to the furthest distance that the winner managed, showing how many children are within the circle and would have been covered in germs.
- Talk to the children about covering their mouth and nose with a tissue to catch the germs and stop the germs from going over their friends.
- Repeat the 'experiment' but this time with the seated child using a tissue to cover their mouth and nose, noting the difference that this makes.

Variations/extensions

- Talk about how just using your hands and not a tissue means the germs are all over your hands and therefore the importance of washing them. This can be linked with 'Pass it on', another activity in this chapter, which deals with germs being passed on and spread by our hands. It can also be linked to responsibility, care and consideration to others

Cross-curriculum link

- Maths

Enamel decay

A simple experiment using eggs and vinegar that shows the effects of plaque and acids on tooth enamel.

Suitable for and curriculum fulfilment

- KS1
- Developing a healthy, safer lifestyle
- To know how to maintain personal hygiene

Aim

- To explain to the children the role of tooth enamel and how, if teeth are not looked after, plaque and acids can damage it

Resources

- Two hard-boiled eggs
- Image of the cross-section of a tooth
- A jar of white vinegar (big enough to put the egg in and remove it easily) labelled 'teeth that haven't been cleaned'
- A similar sized jar of water labelled 'teeth that have been cleaned'
- A spoon to remove the eggs

What to do

- Show the class two hard-boiled eggs.
- Discuss what the shell is for around the egg (to protect the inside).
- Explain that our teeth, like the eggs, are protected with a shell. This shell is called enamel and it protects what is inside our teeth.
- Bring out the two jars.
- Ask two children to place the eggs in the jars and put the lids on.
- Ask what they think will happen to the eggshell.
- Write it down on a large piece of paper and keep it next to the jars on display.

- Two or three days later use the spoon to remove the eggs and compare them.
- Discuss the effects of plaque and acid on our teeth.
- Explain that although we cannot necessarily see that our teeth are dirty we still need to clean them regularly.

Variations/extensions

- Flossing: Tell the children your fingers are teeth. Cover a hand with paint (which represents the food going on to the teeth), making sure to get paint between the fingers. Holding the hand out and keeping the fingers tightly together ask a child to clean the fingers with a damp cloth. After the child has cleaned the hand open the fingers to show the paint between the fingers. Use a strip of material to show how flossing cleans the teeth

Cross-curriculum link

- Science

Let's wash!

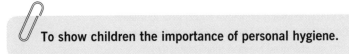

To show children the importance of personal hygiene.

Suitable for and curriculum fulfilment

- KS1
- Developing a healthy, safer lifestyle
- To know how to maintain personal hygiene

Aim

- To show children in a fun way how to wash their hands and to do it for the right amount of time

Resources

- Sink
- Soap
- Towel
- Words of song easily visible

What to do

- Demonstrate the following very slowly with deliberate movements explaining all the various parts. Roll up sleeves, removing any jewellery or a watch.
- Using running hot water; wet your hands and dispense one squirt of the recommended liquid soap or antiseptic into the palm of the hand.
- Hold hands down below the elbow height to prevent water running on to forearms.
- Rub hands together vigorously to lather all surfaces of hands and wrists, paying particular attention to thumbs, fingertips and finger webs.
- Rinse hands thoroughly.

- Turn off water, then dry hands thoroughly on a towel.
- Dispose of the paper towels in the bin (without touching it).
- After explaining how to wash your hands do it one more time, this time singing the song below.
  - It takes about 15 seconds to sing the song, the recommended minimum time you should wash your hands for.
- Observe the children as they take turns to wash their hands.
- When do we need to wash our hands?

Song (To the tune of 'Row, Row, Row your boat')

Wash, wash, wash my hands,
wash the germs away,
scrub and rub and rub and scrub,
I keep them clean all day, HEY!

Wash, wash, wash my hands,
wash the germs away,
scrub and rub and rub and scrub,
I keep them clean all day, HEY!

Variations/extensions

- Getting ready for school, how do we get ready for school?

Sing:

This is the way we brush our hair, brush our hair, brush our hair,
This is the way we brush our hair when we go to school.
This is the way we brush our teeth, brush our teeth, brush our teeth,
This is the way we brush our teeth when we go to school.

Cross-curriculum link

- Science

Pass it on

> This activity is aimed at showing children how germs can be passed on without us realising it and the importance of washing our hands regularly.

Suitable for and curriculum fulfilment

- KS1
- Developing a healthy, safer lifestyle
- To understand how some diseases spread and can be controlled

Aims

- To realise we cannot see germs but it doesn't mean they are not there
- To understand how germs can pass easily if we do not wash our hands
- To understand that by washing and drying our hands properly, far fewer germs will spread

Resources

- Bag or tray of chalk dust
- Two or three pieces of dark coloured card
- Damp/wet cloth
- Dry cloth

What to do

- Sit in a circle on the mat.
- Talk to the children about germs and ask the class if they know what they are and what they do to us.
- Ask the children if they know how they can be spread.
- Get each child to rub their fingertips in chalk dust.
- Pass the dark coloured card around the circle.
- Show the card and explain about germs, dirty hands and how touching things can pass germs around.
- Pass the dry cloth around so each child can clean their hands.

- Pass a second piece of card around the circle, having each child touch it.
- Compare the two sheets of card.
- Show that there are still some marks on the second card.
- Pass the wet cloth around followed by the dry cloth so each child can clean and dry their hands thoroughly.
- Talk to the children about the importance of cleaning their hands thoroughly.

Variations/extensions

- Ask the children to think of other ways germs can spread and what we can do to prevent this

Cross-curriculum link

- Science

Sticker germs

This activity is aimed at showing children how germs can be passed on, can be found where we least expect them and the importance of washing our hands.

Suitable for and curriculum fulfilment

- KS1
- Developing a healthy, safer lifestyle
- To understand how some diseases spread and can be controlled

Aims

- To realise we cannot see germs but it doesn't mean they are not there
- To realise they can be found in places we don't expect
- To understand that by washing and drying our hands promptly and properly, far fewer germs will be spread
- To realise it is not just about hygiene but about caring for your friends and family

Resources

- A sheet of large stickers (low tack)
- Whiteboard or chart

What to do

- Sit in a circle on the mat – late in the morning, before lunch, is best for this activity.
- Talk to the children about germs and how bad they can be for us.
- Ask the children where germs are most likely to be found – the toilet, etc.
- Explain to the children how germs can get on our hands and how it is really important to wash our hands.
- Ask the class whether or not they wash their hands after going to the toilet.

- Ask, 'What if one of us had not washed our hands after going to the loo this morning?'
- Ask the class to describe what they have done today in detail and ask them to place a sticker (or paper with Blu-Tack) on to wherever they put their hands, e.g. door handles, taps, tables, chairs, carpet, books, pens, toys, rulers, boxes, jumpers, faces, friends, etc.
- After a while the room will have stickers all over the place.
- Write the list of places on the whiteboard to reinforce.
- Talk about these places and say that if someone had not washed their hands there would be a germ on all these places.
- Now ask a child to do the things they did in the morning and get the children to call out every time they touch a sticker, marking it on the whiteboard next to the appropriate place.
- Talk about how if there were germs there they would now be on this child's hands.
- Talk about how up to 14 people can catch a germ left on a door handle, etc.
- Talk about the fact that it is not just about hygiene but also about caring for your friends and fellow classmates (you don't want to be the person who made your best friend ill).
- Tell them all to wash their hands before lunch.

Variations/extensions

- Ask the children to think about where else there might be germs. Think of a hospital and why it is important to wash our hands

Cross-curriculum links

- Science
- Maths

Different needs, same needs

This activity is aimed at getting children to recognise the different needs for the different stages and ages in our lives.

Suitable for and curriculum fulfilment

- KS1
- Developing a healthy, safer lifestyle
- To understand the process of growing from young to old and how our needs change

Aims

- To get the children to understand and see that at different ages we all need different things (to go about our daily routines) by linking certain objects to different stages of our lives

Resources

Per group, table or child:

- Five sheets of paper, four sheets each with a different image of a head at the top (a baby, a child, a 'grown-up' and an older person), the fifth sheet with all four images on it
- A sheet of paper with lots of daily objects, e.g. a nappy, a razor, food, a house, a toy, a walking stick, a bike with stabilisers, a bike, a car, toilet paper, toothpaste, homework bag, etc.
- Scissors
- Glue

What to do

- Ask the children who is in their family – their siblings, parent or parents, grandparents, possible uncles, aunts and cousins, their carers, etc.
- Ask how old these people are and try to group them into the four categories on the sheets.
- Ask them to write the names of as many of these people as possible under one of the four corresponding pictures.
- Talk about the stages we go through when we grow up – baby, child, a middle-aged person and an older person.
- Ask what a baby needs that they themselves no longer need.
- Ask what they may need when they get older that they don't need now.
- Ask them to cut out the pictures of these objects and think about which sheet they should go on.
  If they think that more than one group needs the object they can stick it on the 'shared' sheet.
- Ask various children to talk about their sheet.
- Discuss how we need different things throughout different stages of our lives but that we also have constant needs that we share with all our family members.

Variations/extensions

- Homework: Ask the children to create a simple diary chart with the names of their family members. In the boxes next to the names ask them to write things that their family members use

Cross-curriculum link

- Science

Growing up in the park

This activity is aimed at getting children to recognise the different needs and possible activities for different age groups.

Suitable for and curriculum fulfilment

- KS1
- Developing a healthy, safer lifestyle
- To understand the process of growing from young to old and how our needs change

Aims

- To get children to understand that at different ages our interests and activities can change
- To appreciate what we are able to do at different ages

Resources

- Images of different areas of a large well-facilitated park (optional)
- Magazines where children can cut out faces
- A3 sheets of paper
- Glue

What to do

- Encourage the children to talk about older and younger people they know in their family, their neighbours, friends, etc.
- With the teacher leading, start to think of these different ages and think of them as groups: babies, toddlers, children, teenagers, young adults, parents, grandparents.
- Ask the children what different abilities or needs each of these groups have, e.g. can they run, walk, climb trees, go on swings, climbing frames, play football, etc.?
- Talk about a big city park and ask what is in it; show pictures to prompt if necessary.

- Think about all the different areas in this park: different play areas for children, bowling green, boating lake, running track, exercise course, grass area for football/sports, benches, etc.
- Talk about who might like to do what, e.g. teenagers playing sport, older people less active sitting on benches or walking, children in the different aged play areas.
- Get the children working together (in pairs if possible) on an A3 sheet of paper to think of and design a 'Super Park' with different areas for different ages so that all people can use the park and have fun.
- Ask them to find and cut out images (faces only) of different age groups and get them to place these in the most suitable area of the park.
- Ask some of the children to come and talk about their park.

Variations/extensions

- A trip to a well-facilitated park

Cross-curriculum link

- Geography

Body bits

A fun way to find and identify body parts by drawing around the children and by singing.

Suitable for and curriculum fulfilment

- KS1
- Developing a healthy, safer lifestyle
- To know the names of the main parts of the body

Aim

- To be able to recognise and label different body parts

Resources

- Whiteboard with an outline of a girl and a boy
- Continuous white paper (wider than a child)
- Felt-tip pens

What to do

- Bring the children to the mat.
- Stand and sing 'Head, Shoulders, Knees and Toes ... knees and toes'.
- Ask a child to add in extra parts, e.g. 'Head, Shoulders, Elbows, Stomach ... elbows, stomach'.
- Then on the whiteboard ask the children to identify the different body parts.
- Choose a boy and a girl to draw around – the tallest boy and the tallest girl in the class can do this.
- Arrange the children into two groups (boys and girls) and have them label the body parts using the felt-tip pens.

Variations/extensions

- Play 'Simon Says': Simon says 'nod your head ... touch your toes'

Cross-curriculum links

- Science
- Maths

Pin the parts

This activity is aimed at the children being able to identify different parts of the body in a fun way.

Suitable for and curriculum fulfilment

- KS1
- Developing a healthy, safer lifestyle
- To know the names of the main parts of the body

Aim

- To be able to recognise and label different body parts

Resources

- Large sheets of white paper
- Thick black pen
- Cards with names of different parts of the body
- Blu-Tack

What to do

- Ask the children to sit in a circle or on the mat.
- Ask them to identify different parts of the body by pointing to them and writing them on the whiteboard.
- Measure the children back to back to find the tallest boy and the tallest girl.
- Draw around these children on the large sheets of paper.
- Place the outlines on a wall or flat surface (these should be placed at child height).
- Divide the class into two groups.
- Give each child a card to read out, then blindfold the first child and ask them to place the card on the right area of the body.
- Ask each child in the class to have a go.
- When each group has labelled the body outline, ask the children if the cards are all in the right place.

Variations/extensions

- To focus on one particular part of the body or to include placing the major organs

Cross-curriculum links

- Science
- Maths

Don't drink this!

This is a simple way of showing that there are many liquids around the house that can harm if used inappropriately.

Suitable for and curriculum fulfilment

- KS1
- Developing a healthy, safer lifestyle
- To know that all household products, including medicines, can be harmful if not used properly

Aims

- Primarily to show the children the effects of certain common liquids found in the house that can be harmful, by feeding some plants for a week with various household liquids to see how they react
- To introduce to the children some of the less known bottles they may have seen around the house and explain what they should only be used for

Resources

- Three (or more if possible) small indoor plants of the same type that can be left in the classroom
- Common household liquids such as bleach, washing-up liquid, disinfectant, car wash, shampoo, etc.
- Water
- Labels

What to do

Allow this activity to take place during the entire week.

- Ask the children if they have seen these various liquids in their homes and know what they are.
- Ask them if they know what they are for and talk about their uses.

- Explain that all these liquids are really good for doing certain jobs but should only be used for those jobs and that they can be very dangerous if used for the wrong things.
- Talk about water and its uses, including as a drink.
- Ask if we should drink the other liquids. (At this stage emphasise that we should never ever drink any of the above liquids.)
- Explain that you are going to do an experiment to see what happens to the plants.
- Label the plants.
- Every day, twice a day, feed the plants with the different liquids. Over the week see how the plant reacts to the different liquids. Some will die more quickly than others and the one that was fed with water should still be looking good.
- Discuss the conclusions that can be drawn from the activity.

Variations/extensions

- Look at the bigger picture. Discuss what happens when we use weedkiller in our gardens

Cross-curriculum link

- Science

Red Cross box

This simple activity is to introduce and understand why we have a first aid box and what it is used for. It also introduces the children to the main individual items in the kit.

Suitable for and curriculum fulfilment

- KS1
- Developing a healthy, safer lifestyle
- To know that all household products, including medicines, can be harmful if not used properly

Aims

- To understand how we use medicines
- To understand that they should be used with adult supervision only

Resource

- School first aid box

What to do

- Ask the children to sit on the mat.
- Introduce the first aid box.
- Ask the children why there is a red cross on the box.
- Explain the meaning of the mark and that it is used in many different places, not just on a first aid box (give some examples).
- Take the items out of the box one at a time. Ask the children what they think they are used for.
- Explain to the children what they are used for and what could happen if not used properly.

- When all the items from the first aid box are out of the box, ask the children (or one child) to close their eyes and take one item away.
- Ask the children/child what item has been removed and what it is used for.
- Repeat this until all the children know each of the items in a first aid box and their usage.
- Explain why the first aid box should only be used by adults or with adult supervision.

Variations/extensions

- Have a photocopied sheet with the outline of a first aid box on it. Ask the children to draw all the items in it and ask some of them to show the class and tell them what they put in
- Ask a nurse or school medical officer to come in and do the activity

Cross-curriculum link

- Maths

Buckle up

To think about how to travel safely by making seat belts, with notes for parents.

Suitable for and curriculum fulfilment

- KS1
- Developing a healthy, safer lifestyle
- To know rules for, and ways of, keeping safe including basic road safety and about people who can help them to stay safe

Aim

- To understand the importance of seat belts in cars

Resources

- Strips of paper
- A tape measure
- Sticky tape

What to do

- Ask the children if they have ever been in a car.
- Ask where they sit in the car.
- Ask them if there is anything special they need to do when they are in the car.
- Ask how many of them wear seat belts when in a car.
- Ask the children why they think seat belts are important.
- Discuss how seat belts should be worn at all times and any other things that they should or should not do when travelling in a car.
- Write the ideas on the whiteboard.
- Explain to the children that they are now going to make their own safety belts.

- Ask one child to come up to the front so you can show them how to do it.
- Children work together to measure their waists with a tape measure (adding a hand's width to the waist measurement for fastening).
- Ask the children to cut the strips to size, one for the waist and one for going over the shoulder.
- Ask the children to write down all the safety 'rules' as discussed earlier.
- The seat belts are then attached to each child with tape (you will probably need to help with this).
- The children can wear their safety belts home, so the parents or carers can read about car safety.

Variations/extensions

- To role-play, with the children acting as cars and stopping at traffic lights and zebra crossings. This could be done in the playground

Cross-curriculum link

- Maths

Uniforms to help

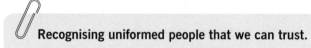

Recognising uniformed people that we can trust.

Suitable for and curriculum fulfilment

- KS1
- Developing a healthy, safer lifestyle
- To know rules for, and ways of, keeping safe including basic road safety and about people who can help them to stay safe

Aims

- To be able to recognise basic uniforms of people we can trust to help us
- To understand what they do and how they can help us

Resources

- Images of local police officers, nurses/ambulance medics and firemen (uniforms can vary between regions)
- Images of them at work and their vehicles
- Craft materials and props to make costume uniforms (if available)

What to do

- Show and talk about these servicemen and women and how to recognise them.
- Ask and discuss what they do, where they work and the kind of situations that end up with their involvement, e.g.
  - Policeman: got lost, a nasty fight, knocked down
  - Nurse/ambulance medic: climbed on roof to get ball back and fell off, knocked down, playing with medicines
  - Fireman: playing with matches at home or in the park.

- Ask groups to make basic costumes based on the details of the uniforms, keeping the pictures up for reference:
  - Policeman: black and white chequered bands, police number, high-visibility vest, black tie, white top/shirt
  - Fireman: yellow hat, black jacket with yellow/grey visibility markings stuck on
  - Nurse/ambulance medic: green and yellow chequered markings, green tops, yellow visibility tops.
- Ask the groups to think of a scenario:
  - What happened?
  - What to do?
  - Which service/services helped and how?
- Ask some children to act out the scenario in front of the class and discuss.
- Discuss what the children should or shouldn't do to avoid these situations and to stay safe.

Variations/extensions

- Think of who else helps us. What would happen if we got lost in the supermarket, or in the park?

Cross-curriculum links

- Art and Design
- Drama

Your local 'Bobby'

To have the opportunity to meet a local police officer/ community police officer who has a visible presence within the local community. This will allow the children to be comfortable in their company, to be able to feel that they can trust them and understand what they do and how they help.

Suitable for and curriculum fulfilment

- KS1
- Developing a healthy, safer lifestyle
- To know rules for, and ways of, keeping safe including basic road safety and about people who can help them to stay safe

Aims

- To be able to recognise basic uniforms of people we can trust to help us
- To understand what they do and how they can help us

Resource

- A local police officer who has a high profile and street presence in the school catchment area

What to do

- Explain and encourage the children to think about the role of a community police officer.
- Prepare some questions with the children to ask the police officer and write them down.
- Try to make the questions as varied as possible:
  - Their day-to-day job
  - The problems in the local area

- How they keep us safe
- Advice for staying safe
- The equipment they carry and use and what it's for
- What they do if a child is lost or hurt and the standard procedures they would follow, etc.
- Send the questions to the police officer in advance so they can be prepared.
- When the police officer arrives encourage the children to engage as much as possible with them, asking further questions and, if permission is granted, handling their equipment and talking about it.
- Ask if it is possible to take a photo of the police officer with the class.
- Print out and place the photo up on the wall in the classroom.
- After the visit, ask the children to write a thank-you letter to the police officer.

Variations/extensions

- Invite a firefighter, nurse, doctor and ambulance driver in for a similar lesson

Cross-curriculum links

- Literacy
- Geography

Look, listen and hold hands

This activity is aimed at showing children why it is important to stop, look and listen when crossing the road.

Suitable for and curriculum fulfilment

- KS1
- Developing a healthy, safer lifestyle
- To know rules for, and ways of, keeping safe including basic road safety and about people who can help them to stay safe

Aim

- To show children why the combination of 'stop, look, listen' is the best and safest way to cross a road

Resources

- Sheets of paper
- A blindfold

What to do

- Lay the paper on the floor to create obstacles to navigate through.
- Choose a child for the task; tell them they must walk five paces without touching any paper and that no child can help them.
- Blindfold the child and get them to attempt the task.
- Talk about how difficult it is when they fail.
- Repeat the task with the blindfolded child but this time get another child to tell them to move left or right or stop, etc.
- Talk about whether listening helped.
- Ask another child to hold the blindfolded child's hand and give them directions as they do it.
- Talk again about how it is still hard, but easier.
- Then ask another child to do it without the blindfold, listening to the other child and using their eyes.

- Ask the child which was the easiest.
- Talk about why it was difficult at the beginning, why it became easier and what combination made it really easy.
- Talk about crossing roads and what they think is the best way to do it.

Variations/extensions

- Draw a map of your local area, showing all the traffic lights, zebra crossings and roundabouts. Ask the children to think about the best areas to cross the road

Cross-curriculum links

- Maths
- Geography

KS2
Ideas

Half empty or half full?

Sometimes in life things do not go your way and you do not get what you want. What can be crucial is how you react to these situations. This activity is designed to show how to deal with negative things that happen in your life and how to try to see things with a positive attitude.

Suitable for and curriculum fulfilment

- KS2
- Developing a healthy, safer lifestyle
- To understand what makes a healthy lifestyle, including the benefits of exercise and healthy eating, what affects mental health and how to make informed choices

Aim

- How you feel about yourself and your life

Resources

- A jug
- A clear glass

What to do

- Show the class a glass and half fill it with water.
- Ask the children if they see this cup as half empty or half full.
- Explain the phrase and that there are different ways to see the same thing in life too.
- Put the children in pairs.
  - One child in the pair will take the role of the grown-up and the other child will play themselves.
  - The grown-up will now tell the child that they cannot go swimmimng.

- The child now has to imagine that this is something that they really wanted to do. How will they react?
- Choose a pair of children to show the role-play.
- Ask the children how they would react.
- Ask the children how they could see this situation differently, e.g. go to park.
- Explain to the children that sometimes we are disappointed when things don't turn out how we want. The most important thing is how we react when things don't turn out the way we expect.
- Make a comparison again with the glass being half empty or half full.

Variations/extensions

- You have lost your Nintendo DS – what do you do?

Cross-curriculum link

- Drama

Recipe for life

Children by now will know they need a healthy diet, but not necessarily what the different foods and their associated groups do for our bodies. This activity is about adding the next layer of understanding.

Suitable for and curriculum fulfilment

- KS2
- Developing a healthy, safer lifestyle
- To understand what makes a healthy lifestyle, including the benefits of exercise and healthy eating, what affects mental health and how to make informed choices

Aims

- To start thinking about their future health and well-being and that healthy eating should be for life
- To create a better understanding of the connection between what food is for and what it does, explaining the different food groups and what the foods are within those groups (see worksheet in the Bespoke resources chapter)

Resources

- Whiteboard
- Worksheet

What to do

- Talk through the worksheet asking the children to fill it out. Worksheet:
  - How old are you?
  - What age would you like to live to?
  - Work out how many years away that is.
  - Can you think of anything with moving parts that we use today that is as old as that?

- Do you think we need to look after our bodies if they are to last as long as that?
- Do you want to stay as happy and healthy as possible all the way through your life?
- What do we need to do to stay fit and healthy now and in the future?
- What is food for? Fill in the outer ring with these answers, starting top left in a clockwise direction.
- Discuss:
  - Protecting our bodies from illness
  - Giving our bodies enough fuel/energy to get us through the day
  - Having strong bones
  - Having energy and potential for growth
  - Being able to build and repair muscles.
- Explain to the class that the food we eat should contain everything our body needs to do these different jobs. We need different things from different foods, as there is no one food that contains everything our bodies need.
- What does it do? Fill in the middle ring with these answers:
  - Vitamins and minerals
  - Carbohydrates
  - Calcium
  - Fats and sugars
  - Protein.
- Fill in the inner box with the correct foods.

Variations/extensions

- Write down what would happen if we only ate mainly sugar
- Write down what would happen if we didn't eat any fruit
- Write down what would happen if we didn't eat any vegetables

Cross-curriculum link

- Science

Bespoke resource

- See worksheet in Bespoke resources chapter at the end of the book

Traffic light labelling

This activity is about getting the children to understand the labelling on packaging and to think about what choices we make when we buy food.

Suitable for and curriculum fulfilment

- KS2
- Developing a healthy, safer lifestyle
- To understand what makes a healthy lifestyle, including the benefits of exercise and healthy eating, and what affects mental health and how to make informed choices

Aims

- To introduce the children to the basics of labelling on food packaging
- To show the children how to make well-informed decisions about food labelling
- To give the children an understanding that a red light on the packaging means the food is high in sugar, fat and salt and that too much is bad for you. An amber light means the food is neither high nor low, so it can be eaten more often, and green is low. So the more green lights the healthier the choice

Resources

- Empty packets of different types of food products
- Use of whiteboard with our recommended daily allowances of sugar, fat, salt
- Three large circles: red, amber, green

What to do

- Ask the children to sit in a circle.
- Place all the packets of foodstuff in the middle of the circle.

- Place the three coloured circles around the outer edges of the circle.
- Explain what the circles mean on the packaging:
  - Red means high in fat, salt or sugar and that too much is bad for you.
  - Amber means the food is neither high nor low in sugar, fat and salt, so can be eaten more often.
  - Green means this is the healthier choice.
- Show the children some of the labels on the packaging.
- Ask if they know the meaning.
- Explain to the children that we have a recommended daily allowance (RDA) of certain minerals, fats, sugar. Then ask the children to decide which circles the food products could be placed in.
- Look at the circles, ask the children what colour gives us our best healthy options.
- Ask the children if it is ever alright to eat food in the red circle (yes, in moderation).

Variations/extensions

- Homework: Look in cupboards at home and write down how many different foods they have in the red, amber and green circles

Cross-curriculum link

- Science

Journey of a germ

The aim of this activity is to get children really thinking about their home environment and the many different ways bacteria germs can move around and how they can end up in our bodies.

Suitable for and curriculum fulfilment

- KS2
- Developing a healthy, safer lifestyle
- To understand that bacteria and viruses can affect health and that following simple, safe routines can reduce their spread

Aims

- To get the children to use their imaginations based on their understanding of where the common breeding places of bacteria are and how they can end up in our bodies
- To get the children to collaborate through teamwork and discussion to produce a creative story

Resource

- Whiteboard with the rules written on it

What to do

- After discussing all the main places, environments and common situations that cause bacteria growth, split the class into groups.
- Tell them they have to come up with the most creative story they can of the life and journey of a bacterium.
- It can be funny and creative but the story must:
  - End up in a human stomach
  - Include how the bacteria were created
  - Describe the journey it took to get into the stomach.

e.g. The boy left the wet football sock on the bathroom floor. The dog picked it up and dropped it by the dog bowl to sniff later. The dog, which didn't eat very nicely because he had lost some teeth, got some of his dinner on the wet sock. Bacteria grew in the creases of this smelly wet sock as it lay there for three days. Mum thought it smelt horrible and picked it up while she was cooking food for lunch and threw it in the bin. She didn't wash her hands and the bacteria went on the plate of food she was making for Grandma. Dad took the plate of food to Grandma and got some on his hands. He went upstairs to give the crying baby the toy she dropped on the floor so she could sleep. The baby put the toy in her mouth and swallowed the bacteria ... she had a bad tummy and cried all night long, along with Grandma, Dad, Mum and the dog!

- After the story is read out to the class, ask how this whole thing could have been avoided at various stages in the journey and what can be learnt.

Variations/extensions

- Ask the children to write and draw their own comic strip

Cross-curriculum links

- Literacy
- Art and Design

Wash your hands

It is important that children know when to wash their hands, and that not doing this affects not just themselves but also those around them. This is a last person standing game that can break up a lesson.

Suitable for and curriculum fulfilment

- KS2
- Developing a healthy, safer lifestyle
- To understand that bacteria and viruses can affect health and that following simple, safe routines can reduce their spread

Aim

- To get children to remember when to wash their hands

Resource

- Space to stand in a circle not too close to each other

What to do

- Talk about how germs spread and explain that one of the main ways to prevent passing germs on and making us ill is by washing our hands before we do certain things.
- Ask the children to stand in a circle.
- Tell them you are going to call out things to do and they have to act it out on the spot as quickly as possible, e.g. go for a swim: moving your arms.
- However, there are certain things you do that mean you need to wash your hands, e.g. eat dinner. For these things you must not do the action for eating but the action for washing your hands.

If you do the eating action, you and the two people on either side have to stand on one leg; they have one chance left!

- The last person standing wins.
- Talk about how your actions affect other people as much as yourself, and the importance of thinking about whether you need to wash your hands or not.

Variations/extensions

- Guess what I am doing: Using action cards, get the children to guess what action you are doing

Cross-curriculum links

- PE
- Drama

Know your parts

This activity is to help children get to know and overcome the embarrassment of learning and using the correct names of the body parts related to puberty by saying them out loud in a group with a simple game.

Suitable for and curriculum fulfilment

- KS2
- Developing a healthy, safer lifestyle
- To understand how their bodies change as they approach puberty

Aims

- To get children to lose any self-consciousness about using the names of the body parts related to puberty
- To get children to know the names and context of the parts

Resources

- Pieces of card with the names of the parts of the body you wish to use
- Pieces of card with the first letter of the words written on

What to do

- Start off by tacking all the cards up.
- Read the names out and explain the meaning in as much detail as you wish.
- Go round the class and ask the children to read out words and ask them if they can remember what they mean.
- Take the words down.
- Have a game by holding up a letter card and asking if anyone can guess which word it is the first letter of.

Variations/extensions

- This can also be done as a quiz with groups of children, giving each team a question at a time and asking different people at the table to give the consensus answer of that table

Cross-curriculum link

- Science

The colourful language of puberty

The aim of this activity is to teach children the names associated with puberty, their meaning and context. This can be done in groups or as individuals.

Suitable for and curriculum fulfilment

- KS2
- Developing a healthy, safer lifestyle
- To understand how their bodies change as they approach puberty

Aims

- To understand the names and words associated with puberty
- To know where these parts are located

Resources

- The words you are using on a whiteboard
- Worksheet: Sentences with gaps missing for the words you wish them to learn
- Two different coloured pens per child

What to do

- Talk about the words in a circle.
- Form groups and ask the children to choose one colour for boys and one colour for girls.
- Ask them to fill in the sentence with the missing words correctly placed using a different colour depending on whether the word relates to a boy or a girl. If the word relates to both boys and girls ask them to write alternate letters of the words with the different colours (have examples on the whiteboard).

Variations/extensions

- A simple drawing of a girl and a boy next to the sentence can be used. Ask the children to draw a line from the word to the area of the body where you would find it
- This can also be used for a lesson on the reproductive process

Cross-curriculum link

- Science

Legal recreational drugs

Introducing the topic of legal recreational drugs with a simple quiz that allows you to discuss and expand in bite-size sections. You should not attempt to scare but educate children. It is about equipping them with the correct knowledge, confidence and skills to deal with situations that arise where they may be present.

Suitable for and curriculum fulfilment

- KS2
- Developing a healthy, safer lifestyle
- To know which commonly available substances and drugs are legal and illegal, their effects and risks

Aim

- To give children a basic knowledge of coffee, alcohol and cigarettes, their effects on the body and why people take them and equipping children with the reasoning to make a sensible decision

Resource

- Ready prepared questions for the whiteboard
  Some examples are given overleaf, some of which are straightforward while others are more open-ended and will involve discussion. Keep it flexible

What to do

- Split the class into groups.
- Explain that we are now going to discover what they know about drugs.
- What are legal drugs?
- What are illegal drugs?
- Are any drugs good for you?

- – For example caffeine, if you were a security guard at night
- – When you are sick.
- Where would you find nicotine?
- In what things would you find alcohol?
- How old do you have to be to buy alcohol?
- How old do you have to be to smoke cigarettes?
- How old do you have to be to drink coffee?
- What parts of the body does smoking damage?
- What is secondary smoke?
- What parts of the body does drinking damage?
- Is it dangerous to drink and drive?
- Is it alright to drink in moderation?

The following questions are more suitable for discussion and also can be written down.

- How do you think cigarettes/coffee/beer/wine can make you feel?
- What does it mean to be addicted?
- Do you think it is good to be addicted?
- Where and when do adults drink alcohol/smoke/drink coffee?
- Recap.

Variations/extensions

- Design a poster illustrating the dangers of smoking
- Role-play peer pressure situations (KS2 3: Learning skills to be assertive and deal with peer pressure; KS2 3: Risk assessment, weighing up the pros and cons)

Cross-curriculum link

- Science

Spiders

This activity is to accompany the definition of what a drug is and is a simple way to introduce children to the concept of how drugs can affect the way you behave and do things. Some experiments were carried out on spiders to see what kinds of webs they would build while under the influence of different drugs. The web page allows you to choose different drugs, legal and illegal, and see the results.

Suitable for and curriculum fulfilment

- KS2
- Developing a healthy, safer lifestyle
- To know which commonly available substances and drugs are legal and illegal, their effects and risks

Aim

- To show children the negative effects drugs can have on you

Resource

- Video link on spiders: http://www.badspiderbites.com/spiders-on-drugs/

What to do

- What are drugs? Ask the children to give their views.
- Then talk about how drugs affect us.
- Are all drugs the same?
- Then show the above link to see the effect drugs have on a spider building its web. (First show the spider when it is not on drugs.)
- Ask the children what the long-term effect on the spider is if it is unable to build its web.

Variations/extensions

- Ask the children to draw a spider's web

Cross-curriculum link

- Art

Action groups

> Judging what kind of physical contact is and isn't acceptable is as much about understanding the emotions and feelings that are behind the action.

Suitable for and curriculum fulfilment

- KS2
- Developing a healthy, safer lifestyle
- To be able to recognise the different risks in different situations and then decide how to behave responsibly, including sensible road use, and judging what kind of physical contact is acceptable or unacceptable

Aims

- To get children to think about how their actions can be seen as a reflection of their emotions
- To learn that there are appropriate and inappropriate actions
- To learn that the way in which you do actions can change their meaning and the response you get dramatically
- To think before you act
- To respect others and think of their feelings

Resources

- A whiteboard with two groups of words:
  - Group 1 Actions: hit, kick, bite, push, hug, cuddle, kiss, etc.
  - Group 2 Descriptors: angry, happy, sad, frustrated, gentle, slow, hard, quick, forceful, nice, horrible, kind, playful, hurts, I don't like, etc.
- Worksheet from Bespoke resources

What to do

- Show the class the words on the board.
- Split the class into groups.
- Ask or tell each group to write one of the action words in the arrow.
- Ask them to discuss and choose which words best describe the feelings of the two people. (The person on the left is committing the action and the person on the right is on the receiving end.)
- They should be encouraged to add words that are not on the list if they want.
- Ask them to show the class and explain their choices.
- Discuss how the person carrying out the action feels and whether it is right or wrong to behave that way.
- Discuss how the other person feels and whether it is important to think about that.
- Talk about respect.
- Discuss thinking before you act.
- By using different descriptors with the action word, often a different story can emerge, e.g. a playful/gentle push is very different from a forceful/angry one.

Variations/extensions

- To add a greater level of complexity by discussing what happens when you change the circumstances and the people involved. For example, pushing a bully away who is hitting you or kissing someone who doesn't want to be kissed. This can become complex and confusing so it is best done when you feel the class is comfortable with the first stage. Alternatively it can be introduced with a particular group who you feel needs a little more of a challenge

Cross-curriculum link

- Literacy

Bespoke resource

- See worksheet in Bespoke resources chapter at the end of the book

Watch out!

Children learn how to weigh up certain risks involved in different situations by role-playing with taking a trip. This will be done using a series of postcards.

Suitable for and curriculum fulfilment

- KS2
- Developing a healthy, safer lifestyle
- To be able to recognise the different risks in different situations and then decide how to behave responsibly, including sensible road use, and judging what kind of physical contact is acceptable or unacceptable

Aim

- To get children to think ahead by planning and considering potential risks and problems

Resource

- Postcards (each with different risks to be written on them once the children have decided where they are going)

What to do

- Tell the children to imagine that they are going to take a trip with some friends.
- Ask the children where they would like to go.
- Ask them to write down and draw a picture of where they have chosen, e.g. going to the beach. This should take the format of a postcard.
- Choose a couple of the replies to discuss further.
- Get the children to think about these trips from beginning to end, to plan an itinerary and look at the risks involved on each of the trips.

- Discuss what they could do in advance to avoid problems or what they could/should do if they find themselves in problem situations, getting the children to role-play wherever possible.
- Ask the children to write home (on the back of their postcards) with a description of where they are and what they did to make the journey safer and with less risk.

Variations/extensions

- To design other postcards for different places they would like to go to and write on the back a description of their journey, highlighting all the precautions they have taken to make it safer

Cross-curriculum links

- English
- Art

Staying strong

Role-play is ideal for a lot of PSHE topics. It's a great way of getting children thinking about, talking through, learning and practising different techniques. The act of having dealt with a situation (albeit within a school classroom) and knowing things to say can be very helpful, as often it's the lack of answers and therefore confidence that can lead to the child relenting. It is important that they feel confident, assertive and not intimidated into making decisions they feel uncomfortable about, which means feeling equipped to be able to deal with these situations.

Suitable for and curriculum fulfilment

- KS2
- Developing a healthy, safer lifestyle
- To understand that pressure to behave in an unacceptable or risky way can come from a variety of sources, including people they know, and how to ask for help and use basic techniques for resisting pressure to do wrong

Aims

- To build confidence and reasoning to deal with any situation
- To feel in control
- To support and feel supported
- To understand that it is OK to be different from other people

Resource

- Props if it is felt helpful

What to do

- Explain that you will be doing some role-play.
- Ask the children to think about a time when they have been put under peer pressure and discuss.
  - It is better that the ideas come from the children, the more relevant to their lives the better, but if there is a certain topic that is current then steer it towards that topic.
- After discussing a handful of ideas develop one or two topics either collectively or in two groups.
- Write a short script about a peer pressure situation including as many ideas for putting pressure on as well as resisting.
- Discuss the situation, any misconceptions about it if relevant and the different feelings and replies.
- At first there should be a lone person resisting.
- Act it out.
- Ask the class about any other possible things that can be said to put pressure on as well as replies for resisting.
- Discuss the different replies and show how they fit into different categories, e.g.
  - Saying why it's a bad idea
  - Saying why you don't want to do it
  - Declaring a simple but confident 'no'
  - Changing the subject to something else to do
  - Not being afraid to repeat your reasons
  - Saying 'goodbye, see you later' and walking away.
- Talk about being strong in yourself and confident that your friends will not think any less of you.
- Redo the play asking a second person to help refuse, supporting the first child.
- Discuss the importance of standing by and supporting friends.
- Talk about positive peer pressure and having friends that you feel comfortable with.

Variations/extensions

- This is also a good one for other PSHE topics:

  3d: Which commonly available substances and drugs are legal and illegal, their effects and risks

  4d: To realise the nature and consequences of racism, teasing, bullying and aggressive behaviours, and how to respond to them and ask for help

  2c: To realise the consequences of anti-social and aggressive behaviours, such as bullying and racism, on individuals and communities

Cross-curriculum link

- Drama

Take the challenge

This quiz is all about getting the children to work in groups to discuss how to stay safe on the internet.

Suitable for and curriculum fulfilment

- KS2
- Developing a healthy, safer lifestyle
- To understand that pressure to behave in an unacceptable or risky way can come from a variety of sources, including people they know, and how to ask for help and use basic techniques for resisting pressure to do wrong

Aims

- To learn the dangers in chat rooms
- To learn how to stay safe
- To learn to consult parents

Resources

- A score card
- Question sheet

What to do

- Talk about the internet and chat rooms.
- Put the children into two or three groups and explain that they have to work together to answer questions about the topic.
  - Which sentence do you think is most true?
    a. All people on the internet are nice
    b. All people on the internet are not nice
    c. There are some nice people and some not so nice people
  - What should you do if you want to join a new chat room?
    a. Ask your mum or dad or guardian first if it's OK to join

    b. Join without telling anyone (mum and dad may not like me joining)

    c. Join first and tell your mum and dad later

    d. Don't join

– What things do you need your mum and dad's permission for?

    a. Opening emails from someone you do not know

    b. Buying things on the internet

    c. Chatting with friends who are on your buddy list

    d. Meeting up with people you have chatted with online

    e. Filling in forms

    f. Entering competitions

– Who can you tell your password to?

    a. Anyone

    b. People you chat with

    c. Your friends

    d. Your parents

– If someone asks you for a photo of yourself, what should you send them?

    a. Your best school photo

    b. A picture of you on holiday looking happy

    c. Nothing. Ask your parents first if it's OK and show them the picture you want to send

    d. A picture of a monkey

– If someone asks you to email them, what should you do?

    a. Email them back

    b. Ask your mum or dad if it is OK

    c. Tell them it's best they phone you and give them your phone number

    d. Show your mum and dad the email you were sent

– If someone tells you they are 9 years old, how old are they?

    a. 25 years old

    b. 9 years old

    c. 55 years old

    d. Could be any age

– Which sentence do you think is most true?

    a. People are always who they say they are on the internet, they don't lie

   b. You can trust anyone on the internet
   c. Everyone lies on the internet
   d. People can pretend to be someone they are not on the internet
- Which of these things can you tell people you chat to without your parents' permission?
   a. Your name
   b. Your age
   c. Where you live
   d. Your password
   e. Your school name
   f. Your telephone number
   g. Your parents' names
   h. The name of any club or team you are involved in
   i. None of these
- What should you do if your chat room friend asks to meet up?
   a. Don't agree. Show your mum and dad and ask them what to do next
   b. Get your coat and go before your mum and dad notice you're missing
   c. Tell them where you live
   d. Give them your email address
- What two things should you do if someone sends you something bad or something that seems wrong?
   a. Tell your parents
   b. Tell them you think it is rude
   c. Stop the chat and log off
   d. Carry on chatting with them
- What two things should you do if someone is rude to you or makes you feel sad or angry?
   a. Tell your parents
   b. Be rude back
   c. Stop the chat and log off
   d. Carry on chatting
- What should you do if someone tells you your best friends or parents are not nice?
   a. Tell them to go away
   b. Don't believe them, they may not be very nice

    c. Ask them why they think that

    d. Ask them to be you friend

– If you come across something rude or bad on the internet, what should you do?

    a. Go back to another page and carry on

    b. Tell your mum or dad. It's not your fault you found this

    c. Show all your friends

    d. Log off or close the computer

- Go through the questions and discuss the answers.

Variations/extensions

- This is a shorter and more narrative led version.
  - You are in a chat room, someone starts talking to you, same age, likes the same music, same taste in film, etc. They ask you if you want to chat by instant messenger. What would you do?

    a. Block them

    b. Stay in the public area of the chat room

    c. Give them your details and add them to your contact list

  - Your friendship with this person continues and they send a photo of themselves. The photo is nice and friendly and looks about your age. They want to see what you look like, what would you do?

    a. Send a photo

    b. Refuse

    c. Say no but carry on chatting

  - You have been chatting for a couple of months now and you get on really well and have loads in common. The person wants to meet you. What do you do?

    a. Meet them in a public place

    b. Tell an adult

    c. Refuse to meet them

  - Plenary

    Go back to the first question – Explain that when you give your MSN details this also links into your email and personal details

    Second question – Once you send a photo you have no control over what that person does with the photo. Also the photo they sent might not be them

Third question – Under no circumstances meet someone you have met from a chat room. You are putting yourself in danger, as they might not be who they say

Cross-curriculum links

- Literacy
- Internet

Time to say 'No'

Learning to say 'No' to things that make you feel uncomfortable is very important. It helps self-esteem and confidence as well as keeping us safe. It is about using your own judgement and feelings to recognise the difference between acceptable and unacceptable requests.

Suitable for and curriculum fulfilment

- KS2
- Developing a healthy, safer lifestyle
- To understand that pressure to behave in an unacceptable or risky way can come from a variety of sources, including people they know, and how to ask for help and use basic techniques for resisting pressure to do wrong

Aims

- To help children recognise that when they feel uncomfortable about being asked to do something unacceptable they should feel confident and not guilty saying 'no'
- To show them that unreasonable requests can come from the least likely of people

What to do

- Gather the children together.
- Ask a child to do something, but only once – maybe 'stand up and stay standing up'.
- Ask another child to do something else – 'stand up and pretend to be a teapot'.
- As you ask different children to do something, make the request more strange – 'stand by the door and put your coat on your head'.
- If a child refuses or hesitates for long enough, say nothing and move on to the next child.

- Keep going until there is a sense of understanding or everyone in the circle has been asked.
- Ask the children to return to the circle.
- Ask how they felt doing the task, and if anyone wanted to say 'no', why they didn't say 'no'.
- Was it right not to do it?
- Discuss:
  - Ways of saying 'no' and how to express why they feel that way
  - Recognising when they feel uncomfortable about being asked to do something unacceptable
  - That they should feel confident and not guilty saying 'no'
  - That unreasonable requests can come from the least likely of people.

Variations/extensions

- Prepare some cards with different scenarios on them. Ask the children in small groups to decide when to say NO

Cross-curriculum link

- Drama

Emergency

This is a simple and fun way to teach children when to dial 999 and what to say.

Suitable for and curriculum fulfilment

- KS2
- Developing a healthy, safer lifestyle
- To know the school rules about health and safety, basic emergency aid procedures and where to get help

Aim

- To know when to call 999 and what they need to say

Resource

- Telephone (unplugged!)

What to do

- Ask them if they know the emergency telephone number.
- Ask them in what situations they should call the emergency services. Discuss their answers and decide which is a good reason and those situations where they shouldn't.
- Discuss what an emergency really is (use basic concepts, like a parent won't wake up, fire, intruder in the house).
- Children should call from the house phone if possible (not a mobile phone as a house phone can be traced).
- The teacher now takes on the role of the operator at the end of the emergency services.
- Encourage the children to speak clearly (children have a tendency to mumble when under pressure).
- The children should learn how to wait on the line, listen and answer questions clearly.

- Run through details like the child's full name, parent's name, house address and directions to the house.
- Stress to the children that they should never dial 999 unless it is an emergency.
- Plenary: Make sure all the children know the emergency number and their important details.

Variations/extensions

- Can they dial 999 with their eyes closed/blindfolded?
- Ask someone to come in and talk about how the call centre works and the kinds of calls they get, both valid and invalid

Cross-curriculum link

- Drama

Read the signs

The activity is for children to understand safety symbols and what they tell us. Teachers need to know the following:

DANGER: Yellow Triangle with a thick black outline indicates warning, e.g. wet floor, hot water, hot surface, fire risk, deep water.

STOP: Red Circle with a line through indicates prohibition, e.g. no parking, no ball games, no entry, no smoking, no access, no running.

OBEY: Blue Circle filled indicates mandatory, e.g. wear gloves, keep shut, keep out, wash hands.

SAFETY: Green Square filled indicates information, safe health and safety place, e.g. assemble, first aid site.

Suitable for and curriculum fulfilment

- KS2
- Developing a healthy, safer lifestyle
- To know the school rules about health and safety, basic emergency aid procedures and where to get help

Aim

- To be able to recognise safety symbols and understand their general and specific meaning

Resources

- Whiteboard with an image of a work place, which could be an office, factory, public place, library or hospital
- Various images of above signs

What to do

- Show the children the different signs/symbols and ask if they know their meanings.
- Start with the colour/shape categories and their general meaning.
- Explain what each sign/symbol means.
- Then have a quiz where each table has to guess what a specific symbol means by the colour, shape and the image inside.
- Take the children on a walk round the school to see what symbols they can identify.
- Once back in the classroom ask the children to think about what signs they might need in a factory, hospital, building site, etc.
- Give them a sheet with black and white logos on and ask the children to label the signs and colour them in with the correct colour (worksheet provided).
- Write examples of where different signs could be used.
- Discuss the activity and their findings as a whole class.

Variations/extensions

- Get the children to design their own safety symbol

Cross-curriculum link

- Art and Design

Bespoke resource

- See worksheets in Bespoke resources chapter at the end of the book

Stop, look and listen

This activity is about developing children's understanding and knowledge of what hazards and what risks they can expose themselves to. It is also about creating a sense of responsibility to others within the school.

Suitable for and curriculum fulfilment

- KS2
- Developing a healthy, safer lifestyle
- To know the school rules about health and safety, basic emergency aid procedures and where to get help

Aim

- To make people aware of road safety

Resources

- A3 paper
- Crayons

What to do

- Ask the children how they should cross a road. (Most children will know from KS1.)
- Ask questions like: And? Then? Why not?
- Ask – When we are crossing the road do we do the following?
  - Talk on our mobile
  - Listen to our mp3
  - Run across the road
  - Wear something bright at night

- Ask how many children have actually run across the road, been pushed into the road by someone else or crossed in a dangerous place.
- Next ask what happens when someone gets hit by a car (answers are likely to include death and various injuries).
- Talk about how drivers break the rules and endanger life. (Driving too fast, talking on mobiles, drinking, parking and dropping off children outside school entrances).
- Talk about speed and speed limits. Does anyone know what the speed limit is outside the school?
- What would happen if you got hit at 20 mph or 40 mph? (If someone got hit at 20 mph they would probably live; at 40 mph they would almost certainly die.)
- Ask how we can get drivers to drive slowly and carefully outside the school by designing a poster. What information would we need?
- Ask the children to design a poster.
- Put posters up around the school and ask some children to speak to the school in assembly about the posters.

Variations/extensions

- Write a letter to parents asking them to drive slowly around the school

Cross-curriculum link

- Literacy

Chapter 4

Developing good relationships and respecting the differences between people

Introduction

Some of the following activities can be used for either KS1 or KS2 but it is really up to the teacher to use their discretion knowing the ability of their class.

There are twelve areas that need to be covered in KS1 and KS2 in this chapter. All the activities have been laid out following this order and below each title is a full description of which one it relates to.

Key Stage 1

Key Stage 1 tackles the children's most immediate environment, creating an awareness of the basic ground rules that are needed to develop and maintain healthy and happy relationships with those who surround them. There are five areas that need to be taught:

- To recognise how their behaviour affects other people
- To listen to other people, and play and work co-operatively
- To identify and respect the differences and similarities between people
- To realise that family and friends should care for each other
- To understand that there are different types of teasing and bullying, that bullying is wrong, and how to get help to deal with bullying.

Key Stage 2

Key Stage 2 develops the themes further and discusses the issues of prejudice and discrimination. It also seeks to challenge and expand on the children's perceptions by exploring the rich and diverse mix of people that live in Britain and around the world. There are seven areas that need to be covered:

- To understand that their actions affect themselves and others, to care about other people's feelings and to try to see things from their point of view
- To think about the lives of people living in other places and times, and people with different values and customs
- To be aware of different types of relationship, including marriage and those between friends and families, and to develop the skills to be effective in relationships
- To realise the nature and consequences of racism, teasing, bullying and aggressive behaviours, and how to respond to them and ask for help
- To recognise and challenge stereotypes

- To understand that differences and similarities between people arise from a number of factors, including cultural, ethnic, racial and religious diversity, gender and disability
- To know where individuals, families and groups can get help and support.

KS1
Ideas

Can't be bothered

This idea is about the consequences of lack of action, encouraging the class to think about how they can affect others as well as themselves.

Suitable for and curriculum fulfilment

- KS1
- Developing good relationships and respecting the differences between people
- To recognise how their behaviour affects other people

Aims

- To get the children to understand that their lack of action can affect themselves and others
- To introduce the notion of collective behaviour

Resources

- Paper and pens

What to do

- Divide the class into as many groups as you want.
- Explain to the class that you are going to talk about an imaginary child, e.g. Billy. Explain that Billy is a child that 'can't be bothered' to do things.
- Tell them you want them to talk about and discuss why Billy should do the things that he doesn't want to do. Start off with ideas where the consequences will more than likely affect just the child:
  - Can't be bothered to do his shoe laces up
  - Or put his coat and hat on on a cold day
  - Or clean his teeth.
- Ask the groups to discuss and write their reasons down.
- Ask the children to stand up and talk about why Billy should do these things and the potential consequences to himself.

- Ask if there are any things that they can think of that sometimes they cannot be bothered to do.
- Move on to actions that will more than likely affect another individual:
  - Can't be bothered to clean up after I spilt a can of sticky drink on a chair
  - Or tidy up the toys on the stairs
  - Or throw litter in the bin as it is too far away (a banana skin).
- Ask the children to discuss and then stand up and talk about their ideas.
- Ask the children if they would like to be the one who sits on the sticky drink or falls on the stairs or has to clean up the mess on the floor if someone else did it. Ask the children how they would feel.
- Move on to actions that can affect our school life, community and/or our planet and how we have a collective responsibility:
  - Can't be bothered to wait my turn in the dinner queue
  - Or close the door, window in winter
  - Or hold the door open for the person following me
  - Or turn the lights /TV off at home.
- Explain that we all have to live together, in families, in communities, as a country and as a planet.
- Explain that our unwillingness to do our bit can affect not just ourselves but also people all around us.
- Talk about how every time we feel we can't be bothered to do something that we know we should, it is important to stop and think about other people and how they would feel.

Variations/extensions

- Not washing hands and leaving germs on shared items for other people, friends and family members to potentially pick up. To be done in conjunction with KS1: Healthy safer lifestyle c: Spreading germs

Cross-curriculum link

- Science

Bespoke resource

- See worksheet in Bespoke resources chapter at the end of the book

Sweets

> This activity creates an example of how someone's selfish impulses can affect others. By discussing the feelings of all involved, the children get to understand the concept of 'fair and unfair' to a greater depth.

Suitable for and curriculum fulfilment

- KS1
- Developing good relationships and respecting the differences between people
- To recognise how their behaviour affects other people

Aim

- To see that our behaviour has consequences for those around us

Resources

- Whiteboard
- A bag of sweets

What to do

- Before the activity take one child away to explain that they are going to take all the sweets as a joke (of course later they will put them back).
- Explain to the children that today we are going to have a special treat as they have all been working very hard.
- Count out the sweets and, together, work out how many sweets each child should take.
- Take the sweets and put them on a table.
- Ask the children to gather around to take their sweets, making sure that the child who is going to take all the sweets is the first in the line.
- What happens when the child takes all the sweets?

- Ask the child to put the sweets back and explain to the class that it is a joke and that you in fact asked the child to take all the sweets.
- Once the children have their share of sweets and are sitting back on the mat, ask them how they felt. Did they think it was fair? Does our behaviour affect other people?

Variations/extensions

- Have a day when everyone keeps smiling. How does it make us feel if we always have a smile on our face?

Cross-curriculum link

- Maths

Thinking of others

> Teaching children that their actions can affect others without their realising it.

Suitable for and curriculum fulfilment

- KS1
- Developing good relationships and respecting the differences between people
- To recognise how their behaviour affects other people

Aims

- To get children to understand that their actions can affect others and make them unhappy
- To get children to think about, discuss and express views as well as to think laterally

Resource

- Sentences written on paper slips to give to the children to read out

What to do

- Tell the children they are going to have a game where they have to guess why the person is sad.
- Choose two children and explain the scenario to them. Give the first child the piece of paper with sentence A. Give the second child the piece of paper with sentence B. Ask the first child to read out sentence A in a happy, excited voice with actions. Then ask the second child to read out sentence B in a sad and unhappy voice with actions.

Scenarios:
On the way home from school
A: happy – 'I like to hide in gardens and jump out and surprise people, it's really fun!'
B: sad – 'Someone keeps coming in my garden and standing on my flowers and killing them. I take a lot of time to look after them.'

In the playground
A: happy – 'We're the oldest in the school and we like to play rough and tumble all round the playground.'
B: sad – 'We don't like to play in the playground because the older children bump into us and knock us over all the time.'

At home
A: happy – 'I like to dance in front of the telly when they show pop videos.'
B: sad – 'I never get to see my favourite band play on the telly because people get in the way.'

In the park
A: happy – 'The park employs someone to keep things tidy so I don't bother putting sweet wrappers and stuff in the bins. There's only one bin in the park – I just throw them anywhere.'
B: sad – 'There are always sticky bits of paper on the slide and the pirate's ship. I got chewing gum all over my trousers once. I had to throw them away.'

In the garden
A: happy – 'I like throwing stones at plastic bottles. I line them up at the end of the garden to see how many I can hit.'
B: sad – 'I don't like to let my cat out into the garden; he came back with a big cut on his head once.'

- Talk and discuss each scenario and how our actions can sometimes affect others.
- Give the children some additional scenarios with 'A' sentences and ask them to think about possible reasons why it may not be such a good idea.

A: 'I like kicking my football against the garage door. It makes a really loud "BANG" when I score!'

A: 'Jumping up and down on my bed is great. I can nearly reach the ceiling!'

A: 'In the park we like to play "tag" ("you're it") in the small kids' playground. There are lots of small kids to run in and out of.'

Variations/extensions

- If you feel they are able to grasp the concept of cycles of behaviour, the following is a nice extension. Ask two children to say their sentence A and B, one after the other, then ask them to repeat them over and over again
  With your brother/sister
  A: happy – 'He called me smelly, so I'm going to call her stinky.'
  B: sad – 'She called me stinky, so I'm going to call him smelly.'
- Talk about how cycles of destructive behaviour can develop if they are not broken

Cross-curriculum link

- Literacy

Co·operation

> This game really forces the children to rely on co-operation, staying calm, good communication, patience and trust in order to win.

Suitable for and curriculum fulfilment

- KS1
- Developing good relationships and respecting the differences between people
- To listen to other people, and play and work co-operatively

Aim

- To learn the skills that are required for good co-operation

Resources

- Blindfold
- Two stools
- A maze drawn on a piece of paper
- Low-tack tape
- Felt-tip pens

What to do

- Organise the children into pairs.
- Blindfold child A and have them sit behind child B with their arms out in front under child B's arms.
- Tape the maze on a wall in front of the children.
- Child A is given a felt-tip pen and has to draw through the maze being guided by child B.
- Ask the other children to watch and learn from the mistakes of the other children so that they can do the task better.
- Let every pair have a go using a different colour felt-tip pen.

▶

276 GAMES, IDEAS AND ACTIVITIES FOR PRIMARY PSHE

- Talk about all the things that they learnt.
- Discuss co-operation on a wider scale and how these principles apply.

Variations/extensions

- This can be done with a game of noughts and crosses with two pairs of children sitting either side of the table

Cross-curriculum link

- Science

In order

This team game relies on co-operation, listening, communication and organisation to win.

Suitable for and curriculum fulfilment

- KS1
- Developing good relationships and respecting the differences between people
- To listen to other people, and play and work co-operatively

Aim

- To learn the skills that are required for good co-operation

Resource

- Three or four blindfolds

What to do

- Divide the class into groups of three or four children.
- Blindfold the children in the first group and ask them to line up in order of age based on birthdays.
- Ask the others to watch and learn how they can do it better when it is their turn.
- Get all the other groups to have a go.
- Talk to the class about all the things that they learnt.
- Discuss co-operation on a wider scale and how these principles apply.

Variations/extensions

- This can be done with larger groups depending on their age and abilities

Cross-curriculum links

- Drama
- Maths

Listening hard

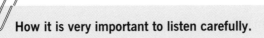

How it is very important to listen carefully.

Suitable for and curriculum fulfilment

- KS1
- Developing good relationships and respecting the differences between people
- To listen to other people, and play and work co-operatively

Aim

- To really listen to our classmates

Resource

- Whiteboard

What to do

- Have the children sit down together on a mat in a circle.
- Ask one child to be your helper.
- Then one by one ask each child how they are feeling.
- Encourage the children to sit very quietly and to listen.
- If someone is feeling sad, encourage the children to ask them why and to listen to their response.
- If someone is feeling sick, encourage the children to ask what is the matter and to listen to their response.
- Likewise, for being tired, or happy, or angry, etc.
- Explain to the children that it is alright to express how we feel and that it is alright to ask how someone is feeling, as this shows that we care.

Variations/extensions

- Start every day by asking each other how they are feeling

Cross-curriculum link

- Science

Teamwork

This team game relies on co-operation, listening, communication and organisation to win.

Suitable for and curriculum fulfilment

- KS1
- Developing good relationships and respecting the differences between people
- To listen to other people, and play and work co-operatively

Aim

- To learn the skills that are required for good co-operation

Resource

- Two large towels per team (or similar material)

What to do

- Create teams of two or three children (depending on the size of your towels).
- Give each team two towels.
- Create a starting line and finishing line at least five towel lengths away from the start.
- Give the children a scenario, e.g. 'they are on one side of a dangerous river with nasty crocodiles that will eat them if they enter the water. They have to race each other to get to the other side. They have magic towels to lay out over the river to get them to the other side but they have to be careful, they must do it without stepping off the towels and stepping in the water.'
- Explain the rules:
  - Each team has to cross the river at the same time
  - They must lay the towels out on the floor, one after the other, to reach the other side

– If one of the team steps in the water that team is out of the game.
- Discuss what they needed to do to win the race.
- Discuss how they had to work as a team and how sometimes working together is the best way to do things.
- What are the key things they needed to do to get across? Listen, share the work, help each other, let other people take responsibility for different parts of the task, stay calm, etc.
- Discuss co-operation as a wider theme and how these principles apply.

Variations/extensions

- This can be done with larger groups depending on the size of the material used

Cross-curriculum link

- PE

Runaround

This activity is aimed at getting children to recognise that other children in their class have similar and different likes.

Suitable for and curriculum fulfilment

- KS1
- Developing good relationships and respecting the differences between people
- To identify and respect the differences and similarities between people

Aims

- To get the children to see that within their class children can have different likes and dislikes
- To apply this to a bigger picture

Resources

- Ideally a playground or an empty hall
- Hoops that you can label with the words 'Like', 'Dislike' and 'Don't Know'

What to do

- Ask the children to write one thing they like and one thing they dislike on separate pieces of paper, e.g. a television programme, a food, a pop star, a hobby, a sport, an animal, a favourite day out.
- Gather the lists.
- Go into the playground or open space.
- Place three hoops on the floor apart from each other, each labelled with one of the words 'Like', 'Dislike' and 'Don't Know'.

- Read out the things the children wrote down one by one, asking them to run to the marker that best represents their feelings about each item.
- After each change quickly observe and mention the names of the children who are now in the same groups or are now in different groups.
- It is a good opportunity to try to pick out two children who do not get on so well and show how they can like the same things and how people who do get on well may not like the same things.
- Discuss that we all have different likes and dislikes.
- Explain that this is normal and that we should be confident in what we like and dislike because we all like different things.

Variations/extensions

- Create a simple chart that allows the class to see that we all like different things

Cross-curriculum links

- PE
- Literacy

My flavour

A simple game to help find out about our classmates, what we have in common, our differences, likes and dislikes. This can be applied to all sorts of topics.

Suitable for and curriculum fulfilment

- KS1
- Developing good relationships and respecting the differences between people
- To identify and respect the differences and similarities between people

Aim

- To find out about our classmates and to find out what things we have in common and our differences

Resources

- None needed

What to do

- This is a take on the old memory game of 'I went to the shops and I bought ...'
- Ask the children to sit in a circle.
- Explain that the class is going to play a game to find out in what way we are different and in what way we are the same, by finding out our favourite ice cream (make sure in advance that each child likes ice cream or is allowed to eat ice cream).
- The teacher is to start.
  - Hello, my name is Mrs McCormick and I like mint chocolate ice cream.
  - The next child (e.g. Julie) will say: Mrs McCormick likes mint chocolate ice cream and I like strawberry ice cream.

> - The next child will say: Mrs McCormick likes mint chocolate ice cream and Julie likes strawberry ice cream and I like chocolate.
> - The game continues, getting harder and harder!
> - Who liked the same ice cream? Can anyone remember?
>   - So do we all have to like the same ice cream?
>   - Isn't it great that we all like ice cream and some of us like the same flavours and some of us like different flavours?

Variations/extensions

- Create a simple chart that allows the class to see that we all like different things

Cross-curriculum link

- Drama

Stand up, sit down

This game is a quick, fun way to introduce the topic of the similarities and differences between people.

Suitable for and curriculum fulfilment

- KS1
- Developing good relationships and respecting the differences between people
- To identify and respect the differences and similarities between people

Aim

- To begin to see the similarities and differences between the children within the class

Resources

- A simple story tailored to include a lot of relevant descriptions about the children in the class.

The story

Adam *is a boy* and has *brown hair*, *green eyes* and *loves football*. His *favourite food is pasta* but he also really *likes chocolate*. He *has a sister* who *loves wearing dresses*; her *favourite colour is blue*. Their *mum and dad are from Pakistan* but they were *born in Birmingham*. Adam's best friend is Malcolm; he has *red hair* and likes to *ride his bicycle*.

After Adam and Ada's father has *been to the mosque* on Friday they *like to buy an ice cream* and *go to the park* to *meet their friends* Malcolm, Jo and Jenny. They all *have uniforms* on because they are *going to the local church* where the *Cub Scouts* and *Girl Guides* meet. *They like to go on the swings.* Jo has *freckles* and has *blond hair* and *likes playing with her friends*. Ada likes Jo's freckles and Jo likes Ada's beautiful dresses. Jenny *wears glasses* and *likes wearing jeans* ... etc.

It is a good idea to finish the story with a description that all the children can identify with

What to do

- Tell the children you are going to read a story.
- Tell the children that when they hear something that describes something in common with themselves they should stand up, e.g. their hair, eyes or what they wear, something about their family, something they do or something they like.
- Tell the children that when they hear something being described that doesn't describe themselves then they should, if they are standing, sit down. For example: 'The brown-haired' (wait for brown-haired children to stand up) 'boy' (wait for the girls to sit down) likes to buy ice creams (wait for them to stand up or sit down).
- The reading of the story can be done playfully so that the children are happy to listen and have some fun.

Variations/extensions

- Create a simple chart that allows the class to see that we all like different things

Cross-curriculum links

- Literacy
- Maths

Care

A short simple circle time idea to introduce the concept of care.

Suitable for and curriculum fulfilment

- KS1
- Developing good relationships and respecting the differences between people
- To realise that family and friends should care for each other

Aim

- To understand what care is

Resources

- None needed

What to do

- What happens when you cut and hurt yourself?
  (You need to put a plaster on to protect you and make you better again.)
- Explain to the class that we can also feel hurt inside when we are upset, worried or sad (e.g. someone was horrible to you.
- Explain that there aren't any plasters in the cupboard at home that we can use for that.
- What do you think you need to help you feel better? Give the class some examples of situations and ask them what would make them feel better.
  - What might you need when you're feeling scared? Being given a hug.
- Explain that there is a thing that we all have that we can give to make each other feel better. Care.

- What is care?
- Care is like a big invisible plaster that we can wrap around people that helps protect them and makes them feel better.
- It is doing all the things for other people that we want other people to do for us.
- Give some examples:
    - It's when you notice a friend is upset or hurt and you stop to help them
    - Maybe it's giving a hug to a friend when they are hurt
    - It's helping someone pick up some things they have dropped
    - It's helping out around the house.
- Explain to the class that it is important that we all show care to each other and look after each other.

Variations/extensions

- Discuss all the people in the community that having 'caring' jobs

Cross-curriculum link

- Literacy

Who do we care for?

A simple activity that introduces the idea of care and how they should treat one another.

Suitable for and curriculum fulfilment

- KS1
- Developing good relationships and respecting the differences between people
- To realise that family and friends should care for each other

Aim

- To think about those who we should care for

Resource

- Heart-shaped paper for each child

What to do

- Introduce the word 'care' and discuss what it means.
- Give examples of situations where we should care for our friends and family, e.g.
  - When you notice a friend is upset or hurt and you stop what you are doing and go up to them and help them.
  - Giving a friend a hug when they are sad.
  - Sharing your snack with a friend if they are hungry.
  - Giving your mum a hug and telling her you love her when she is not feeling well.
- Discuss the words that describe care:
  - Respect, looking after, kind, love, friendship, support, hugs, giving, sharing, listening, and helping.
- Talk about how it is important that we care for each other and help each other.

- Give each child a heart-shaped piece of paper.
- Tell them that the heart represents caring.
- Ask the children to write the words that represent care around the inner edge of the heart-shaped paper.
- Explain that these are the things we need to do to keep our friendships happy.
- Ask the children to write the names or draw pictures of the people they care about in the middle of the heart-shaped paper.
- Encourage the children to take them home to hang up in their bedrooms.

Variations/extensions

- Make a classroom display using all the love hearts

Cross-curriculum links

- Literacy
- Art

Working together

> The idea that working together results in a successful outcome.

Suitable for and curriculum fulfilment

- KS1
- Developing good relationships and respecting the differences between people
- To realise that family and friends should care for each other

Aim

- To recognise how we are stronger when we work together

Resources

- Whiteboard
- A ball of string

What to do

- Ask the children what job a fisherman does on a boat. Does everyone do the same job?
- List all the jobs you would need to do on a fishing boat.
- Ask the children whether if they didn't work together they would be able to catch any fish.
- Show the children a piece of string.
  - Is it strong?
  - Can it be easily cut?
- Cut the string with a pair of scissors.
- Take three pieces of string and show the children how to plait the string.
  - Now can it be easily cut?
  - Let's try.

- Ask the children to practise plaiting the string.
- Plenary
  - What happens when we work together? We are stronger.

Variations/extensions

- Try this activity with a piece of paper; one sheet can easily rip but a whole pad is much harder to tear

Cross-curriculum link

- Maths

An apple

By using an apple we can show children that when we say hurtful things we often hurt other people inside but not notice any difference on the outside.

Suitable for and curriculum fulfilment

- KS1
- Developing good relationships and respecting the differences between people
- To understand that there are different types of teasing and bullying, that bullying is wrong, and how to get help to deal with bullying

Aim

- To show that inside we feel bruised or hurt when people say things that are not nice

Resource

- Two apples

What to do

- Ask the children to sit in a circle.
- Ask the children how they feel when something is said to them that isn't nice.
- Ask them if we always show what we feel on the outside if we are being bullied or teased.
- Teacher to start by thinking of, and sharing with the class, something that has been said that has made him/her feel bad.
- Now ask the children to pass around one of the apples and to think of something that has been said to them that isn't nice and then to hit the apple on the floor.
- Continue around the circle until every child has had a turn.

- Now cut the two apples in half.
- Pass around the cut apples so the children can see that the apple that was used appears bruised and damaged on the inside (wait for the bruises to appear).
  - This illustrates what happens when we say hurtful things.

Variations/extensions

- Pass around another apple, taking care not to drop it, and ask the children to take turns to say positive things

Cross-curriculum link

- Drama

Bullying box

To encourage children who are being bullied to write down their feelings, describing how they are being bullied.

Suitable for and curriculum fulfilment

- KS1
- Developing good relationships and respecting the differences between people
- To understand that there are different types of teasing and bullying, that bullying is wrong, and how to get help to deal with bullying

Aim

- To give children an outlet to express how they feel about bullying

Resource

- A box

What to do

- Ask the children what bullying is.
- Explain that bullying is the conscious desire to hurt, exclude or put someone else down to make the bully feel better.
- Ask the children what type of person bullies.
- What things do bullies do? Some of the answers could be:
  - Constantly ignoring someone
  - Excluding someone from the group
  - Spreading rumours about someone
  - Making fun of someone.
- Ask the children to write down some bullying actions:
  - Teasing
  - Mean words
  - Name calling

- Hitting
- Pushing.
- Ask the class how we help the bullies in their bullying:
  - By providing an audience
  - By not supporting someone who is being bulled
  - By passing on rumours
  - By laughing or joining in.
- Show the children the box.
- Explain that if anything happens they can write about it and put it in the box.
- Place the box somewhere in the classroom.
- At the end of the day read any notes that have been placed in the box.
- Explain to the children what will happen in response to any notes received:
  - Respect confidentiality (if requested) – this might need an explanation, e.g. no one will tell who has written the note
  - Investigate
  - Give advice
  - We will listen sympathetically and carefully
  - Your problem will be taken seriously
  - We will suggest ways of going forward
  - We will support you
  - The class will support you.

Variations/extensions

- Have a Positive box and encourage the children to write about positive actions done by themselves or a fellow classmate

Cross-curriculum links

- Drama
- Literacy

Help me

A good way to get children to discuss and talk about bullying. Through finding out what is wrong with a sad puppet the children learn about bullying and find out what they can do to stop it.

Suitable for and curriculum fulfilment

- KS1
- Developing good relationships and respecting the differences between people
- To understand that there are different types of teasing and bullying, that bullying is wrong, and how to get help to deal with bullying

Aims

- To learn about the different kinds of bullying
- To see how bullying affects people
- To learn what you can do if you are being bullied

Resources

- A puppet
- Types of bullying:
  http://www.bullying.co.uk/index.php/young-people/advice/introduction-to-bullying.html
- How does it make you feel?
  http://www.bullying.co.uk/index.php/parents/is-child-bully/how-does-bullying-make-a-child-feel.html
- What can you do to stop it?
  http://www.direct.gov.uk/en/YoungPeople/HealthAndRelationships/Bullying/DG_10031374
- Other helpful pages:
  http://www.direct.gov.uk/en/YoungPeople/HealthAndRelationships/Bullying/DG_10031370
  http://www.bullying.co.uk/index.php/schools/general/school-projects.html
  http://news.bbc.co.uk/cbbcnews/hi/specials/bullying/default.stm

What to do

- Tell the class you are going to have one of your friends come in and you haven't seen them for a long time.
- Introduce your puppet, making him look sad.
  - I thought you'd be happy to see me? Why are you so sad?
- The puppet is not so forthcoming with saying anything so the children and the teacher need to coax the information out (if you feel silly doing a voice, get the puppet to whisper in your ear).
- Get the class to ask questions to find out what is wrong with 'Bobo'.
- Break the conversations into five parts:
  Part 1 – The different ways Bobo is being bullied
  Part 2 – How it makes Bobo feel
  Part 3 – Is it right or wrong? Why?
  Part 4 – What can Bobo do to stop it?
  Part 5 – Has it helped Bobo talking to the class, and what is Bobo going to do about it?
- Always keep the class involved by asking what they think or their advice or if they know of or have heard anything about being bullied, how it makes you feel, what to do, etc.
- Get the puppet to thank the class.

Variations/extensions

- Get Bobo back in to talk about how his life has turned around after sorting out the problem. What did he do? How does he feel now? Does he wish he had dealt with it earlier? What advice would he give?

Cross-curriculum link

- Drama

KS2

Ideas

A drop

To listen to a song about individuals making a difference and understand that our actions, however small, affect ourselves and other people.

Suitable for and curriculum fulfilment

- KS2
- Developing good relationships and respecting the differences between people
- To understand that their actions affect themselves and others, to care about other people's feelings and to try to see things from their point of view

Aim

- To be able to understand that their actions affect themselves and people around them

Resource

- http://www.youthmusic.org.uk Drop in the Ocean

What to do

- After listening to the music discuss the following points (these have been adapted from the website).
- How can the lyrics of 'Drop in the Ocean' celebrate the impact that young people can have as individuals? The oceans can be seen as communities.
Read out the lyrics to the song again.
The lyrics of 'Drop in the Ocean' celebrate the impact that young people can have as individuals.

> Drop, drop, drop in the ocean
> Drop, drop, drop in the ocean
> Drop, drop, drop in the ocean
> Drop, drop, drop in the ocean.

- Then fill up a very large bowl or water in a sink and take a tissue and squeeze one drop on to the still surface of the water.
- What happens?
- How does this link to the song?
- Discuss together.

Variations/extensions

- Discuss a more global impact, i.e. what happens when we leave the tap running?

Cross-curriculum links

- Literacy
- Music

Point at me

> To play a game (choosing the most confident children in the class) by putting cards on their backs, with words or sentences, like 'Point at me', 'Laugh at me'.

Suitable for and curriculum fulfilment

- KS2
- Developing good relationships and respecting the differences between people
- To understand that their actions affect themselves and others, to care about other people's feelings and to try to see things from their point of view

Aim

- To be able to feel what it is like and to empathise with other people

Resource

- Cards with negative actions, 'Point at me', 'Laugh at me', 'Hum when I am talking'

What to do

- Choose four children from the class (make sure they are confident).
- Explain to the class that we are going to attach cards to their backs.
- Ask the class to follow what the card is asking them to do:
  - Laugh at me
  - Ignore me
  - Hum to me
  - Pull faces at me.
- The children wearing the cards are to find out what is on the card they are wearing.

- Ask the child how they felt.
- Was it nice?
- Can we imagine how it would have felt?

Cross-curriculum link

- Literacy

Setting an example

This fun puzzle shows how we all learn to do things by watching other people, and the importance of our own actions and setting good examples.

Suitable for and curriculum fulfilment

- KS2
- Developing good relationships and respecting the differences between people
- To understand that their actions affect themselves and others, to care about other people's feelings and to try to see things from their point of view

Aim

- To get children to think about their behaviour and how their actions are setting examples to other children around them

Resources

- http://www.youtube.com/watch?v=y9kKHoAPa6A
- http://easybartricks.com/bar-magic.html
- Props relevant to the puzzle/trick

What to do

- Set up and explain the puzzle.
- Ask one child to come up and try to solve the puzzle.
- Show them how to do the puzzle.
- Ask someone else to try to solve the puzzle.
- Ask how they knew how to do it (by copying the teacher).
- Ask the class if there are a lot of things we learn this way (by seeing how other people do things).
- What examples can the class give?
- What about the way we treat people? Do we learn how to treat people by the way we see others, especially our friends and those we look up to, treat people?
- Does anyone have any examples?

- What about the way we behave? Do you think there are children learning from us (e.g. younger children or friends)?
- Whether we realise it or not we all watch each other.
- This means other children are watching us, especially our friends, and they will copy the things we do and the way we treat people, both good and bad.
- Do you think it is important that we treat other people nicely so that they will learn to treat us the same way?
- Do you think it is important to set a good example?
- So try to think about the way we behave and how that affects the way other people behave.

Cross-curriculum link

- Science

Earning your keep

> To look at one aspect of children's lives in different times and places.

Suitable for and curriculum fulfilment

- KS2
- Developing good relationships and respecting the differences between people
- To think about the lives of people living in other places and times, and people with different values and customs

Aim

- To think about themselves by comparing their lives with those of other children past and present

Resources

This activity requires quite a lot of preparation as each of the cards needs to be prepared beforehand

- World map
- Cards with gender, age, how many years ago, what job they did, where they were, e.g.

Boy
- 8 years old
- 200 years ago
- Fighting in a war (at sea)
- Trafalgar, Spain, Europe

Girl
- 8 years old
- 150 years ago
- Chimney sweep
- London, England, Europe

Boy
- 6 years old
- 100 years ago
- Emperor of all China
- Peking, China, Asia

Girl
- 8 years old
- 3500 years ago
- Working in the kitchen, doing household jobs
- Memphis, Egypt, Africa

Boy
- 8 years old
- 2300 years ago
- Becoming a warrior
- Sparta, Greece, Europe

Girl
- 9 years old
- Now
- Sorting out (rubbish on rubbish dumps)
- Payatas dump, Philippines, Asia

Boy
- 8 years old
- Now
- Digging (in mines)
- Tongoma, Sierra Leone, Africa

Girl
- 8 years old
- 2000 years ago
- Slave
- Rome, Roman Empire, Europe

Girl and Boy
- 8 years old
- Now
- Don't need to work!
- England, Europe

What to do

- Ask a child to come to the front and pick a card.
- Tell them you are going to have a game based on guessing what children have had to do as a job at their age.
- Tell the class the main headings, i.e. age, gender, etc.
- Get the class to ask questions and see if they can guess the job.
  - The child is allowed to act things out and say yes or no.
  - They can give actions if it helps, as in higher or lower for the number of years ago, etc.
  - They can point at the map too, with the help of the teacher if required.
- After each one, have a short discussion about their jobs and conditions.
- You can do as many as you wish.

Variations/extensions

- Look in depth at some of the jobs. Ask small groups to research a different one each on the internet and give a short talk about their person to the class

Cross-curriculum links

- Geography
- History

Greetings

To look at the many different ways cultures greet and say hello. Each meaning may reflect something different in each culture but all greetings are about mutual respect in one form or another.

Suitable for and curriculum fulfilment

- KS2
- Developing good relationships and respecting the differences between people
- To think about the lives of people living in other places and times, and people with different values and customs

Aim

- To think about the different meanings behind the way we greet each other around the world

Resources

- World map with photo of a person from each country
- http://www.elephantjournal.com/2010/08/stick-your-tongue-out-at-tibetans/
- Cards with different instructions on how to greet each other:
  - Tibetans: stick your tongue out and show it to the other person
  - Japanese: bow to the other person (with your arms by your side if you are a boy and with your hands held in front of you if you are a girl)
  - Kunik (Alaska): press your nose against the cheek or forehead of the other person
  - Maori (New Zealand): rub your nose against the other person's nose
  - French: kiss both cheeks of the other person
  - Hindus (India): press your hands together over your heart

What to do

- Ask the class how they greet each other.
- Tell them that around the world there are many traditional ways to greet each other.
  (A lot are disappearing as the handshake becomes more common.)
- Can they guess which person from which country uses which greeting?
- Get a pair at a time to come up to the front of the class.
- Give them a card with instructions on and ask them to perform the greeting.
- Get the children to guess where the greeting is from.
  - Repeat until all the greetings are completed.
- Ask them how it felt doing the different greetings. Was it comfortable or uncomfortable, etc.?
- Did they know some cultures do not even touch each other when they meet and would feel uncomfortable shaking hands?
- Why are there different greetings?
  - The Japanese bow is about respect
  - The Kunik and Maori greeting is about closeness and affection
  - The Tibetan sticks his tongue out to show you he is an honest person
  - The Hindu greeting, namaste, means 'I bow to you' or 'I'm humble in your presence'
- Greetings can be about mutual respect.
- Ask the children which was their favourite greeting and why.

Variations/extensions

- What about our verbal greetings? How can we say hello in different languages?
- How do other people say hello to each other?
  - Maori: 'Be well/healthy'
  - In Swahili: 'What is the news?'
  - Rural Tahiti: 'Where are you going?'
  - Muslims: 'Peace be upon you'
  - In Yiddish: 'May peace be unto you'
  - Botswana: 'How did you wake?'

- Georgia: 'Let you win'
- Iceland: 'Happy'
- Mauritania: 'On you no evil'
- Niue, Polynesia: 'Love be with you'
- Swaziland: 'I see you!'
- Malaysia: 'Where are you going?'
- Tawain: 'Have you eaten yet?'

Greetings are about people showing respect, interest, concern and affection and wishing the best for friends and other people. Ask them why they think the Taiwanese say: 'Have you eaten yet?'

Cross-curriculum link

- Geography

My day

To look at children going to school in different countries and their family life.

Suitable for and curriculum fulfilment

- KS2
- Developing good relationships and respecting the differences between people
- To think about the lives of people living in other places and times, and people with different values and customs

Aim

- To think about different places and about children who are at school in different situations

Resource

- http://www.oxfam.org.uk/coolplanet/kidsweb/wakeup/index.htm

What to do

- Look at the stories of the children from the website together.
- Encourage the children to think about what life is like for other children who go to school.
- Look at the pictures of the four children who go to school.
- First let's talk about Anusibuno, who lives in Ghana.
  - Why do her friends not go to school?
  - How does Anusibuno make her toys?
- Next let's talk about Sasha who lives in Siberia in Russia. They grow vegetables and his stepfather works in a coal mine.
  - Do you know if there are any coal mines in the UK?
  - What is the weather like where Sasha lives?

- Cidinha lives in Brazil.
  - What language does she speak?
  - What do you think the effects of a weak electricity supply and power cuts are for her and her family?
  - How does she feel about going to school?
- Finally Shakeel lives in India, which is the most populated country in the world.
  - How many languages are spoken in India?
  - Do they wear shoes to go to school?
  - What do his friends wear?

Variations/extensions

- Imagine you are a school from 100 years ago. Have the children working on slates and learning the 3 Rs

Cross-curriculum link

- Literacy

Our fair share

A simple little analogous game that demonstrates that to make relationships work requires equal amounts of effort from both sides.

Suitable for and curriculum fulfilment

- KS2
- Developing good relationships and respecting the differences between people
- To be aware of different types of relationship, including marriage and those between friends and families, and to develop the skills to be effective in relationships

Aim

- To start a debate about relationships and what is required to make them work

Resources

- None needed

What to do

- Sit two children back to back on the floor and ask them to stand up at the same time.
- Discuss how they did it.
- Ask them to do it again two or three times.
- Talk about how both had to put in the same amount of effort and trust the other person to do the same (how it took a little while to get it right and find the balance, feel what the other person was doing and respond and how much easier it was the more they did it).
- Ask them to do it again, but this time one putting more effort in than the other, and then swap roles.

- Talk about how much harder it is when the other person doesn't do their bit.
- Talk about how this applies to relationships.
- Discuss friendships and the kinds of things that people need to do to make a happy and fulfilling friendship, e.g. showing and giving each other equal respect, time and help.
  - Talk about sharing, co-operation and fairness.

Variations/extensions

- A whole class has a stick, a long stick; half the class stand on one side and the other half on the other. They have to get the stick down to the floor without taking their fingers off it

Cross-curriculum link

- Drama

The 3 Rs of a relationship

> The 3 Rs of a relationship: roles, rules and rituals. This topic discusses different relationships and how they differ using the 3 Rs.

Suitable for and curriculum fulfilment

- KS2
- Developing good relationships and respecting the differences between people
- To be aware of different types of relationship, including marriage and those between friends and families, and to develop the skills to be effective in relationships

Aims

- To start a debate about relationships and what is required to make them work
- To identify different kinds of relationships

Resources

- Prepared worksheet (with: Parent/Guardian, Best friends, Other children, Teachers across the top; and Roles, Rules, Rituals down the side)
- Whiteboard with worksheet on

What to do

- Explain to the children what the 3 Rs to a good relationship mean.
  - The 3Rs to a good relationship = roles + rules + rituals
  - Explain and discuss what each word means.
  - **Roles**
  Different things you should do for each other, e.g. with parents:
  - What's expected of you – listen to your parent, follow house rules and help out

- What's expected of the parent – look after you, help you, keep you safe, love you and tell you off if you are naughty

Rules

How you treat each other, e.g.

- Share
- Be kind
- Care for
- Help out
- Respect
- Be considerate

Rituals

Things you should do regularly together, e.g.

- Spending time together doing things that remind you how well you get on
- Saying hello, thank you and goodbye, hugging, letting each other know how much you love each other

- Talk about different kinds of relationships – parents/guardians, best friends, other children, teachers, etc.
- Show them the worksheet.
- Discuss.
  - Ask them if they can give any good or bad examples.
- Ask the children to fill in their own sheet, putting in words and phrases that apply for them.

Variations/extensions

- In pairs, role-play with one being the parent and one being the child

Cross-curriculum links

- Literacy
- Drama

Bespoke resource

- See worksheet in Bespoke resources chapter at the end of the book

Together

The different relationships that people have.

Suitable for and curriculum fulfilment

- KS2
- Developing good relationships and respecting the differences between people
- To be aware of different types of relationship, including marriage and those between friends and families, and to develop the skills to be effective in relationships

Aim

- To explore the different types of relationship and the different factors that help form relationships

Resource

- Clippings from magazines, to highlight some relationships

What to do

- Look at the clippings together.
- Talk about the different relationships people have.
- Discuss the different types of relationship – relationships we have with our family, relationships we have with our friends and when we are older relationships we have with someone else.
- What are the most important factors in forming a relationship? Focus on a couple who have just married and another couple who have just got engaged (or just got together).

- – Have they got similar interests (these can be highlighted before the lesson, e.g. they both play tennis, listen to the same type of music)?
  - – Is this enough?
  - – Is it important that they do things together?
  - – Is it important that they share problems with each other?
- What is important in our relationship with friends?
  - – How do they make us feel happy?
  - – Is it important for our friends to be similar?
  - – Do our friends share our experiences?
  - – Do our friends give us support?
- Finally we can look at relationships within the family.
  - – Do we need to work at relationships with the family?
  - – Should our family always there for us?
  - – How should we treat members of our family?
- Ask the children to write down what a relationship means to them and what they expect in a relationship.
- Why do relationships go wrong?
  - – Is it abuse of trust?
  - – Lack of communication?
  - – Conflict?
- Ask the children to think about all these things and then to write what is important to them in a relationship.

Variations/extensions

- Discuss the last Royal Wedding

Cross-curriculum link

- Literacy

Get to know about bullies

This activity encourages the class to learn about bullying and all it entails through research and discussion.

Please look thoroughly at all these websites and make sure you feel comfortable with all the information on them and the possible questions or issues they could bring up.

Suitable for and curriculum fulfilment

- KS2
- Developing good relationships and respecting the differences between people
- To realise the nature and consequences of racism, teasing, bullying and aggressive behaviours, and how to respond to them and ask for help

Aims

- To encourage children to research issues that may affect them
- To teach them a good awareness of the different types of bullying
- To help them know what to do if they or someone they know is being bullied
- To work co-operatively

Resources

- IT room with internet access
- Website pages to start with:
  http://www.childline.org.uk/Explore/Bullying/Pages/Bullying.aspx
  http://www.direct.gov.uk/en/YoungPeople/HealthAndRelationships/Bullying/index.htm
  http://www.bullying.co.uk/index.php/young-people/advice/introduction-to-bullying.html
  http://www.bullying.co.uk/index.php/parents/is-child-bully/how-does-bullying-make-a-child-feel.html
  http://www.pacerkidsagainstbullying.org/ (go to 'watch this' then 'kids vids')

- List of questions:
  - What are the different ways of being bullied?
  - Why do bullies do it?
  - How does it make the person feel?
  - Is it right or wrong? Why?
  - What can you do to avoid it or stop it?

What to do

- Split the class into small groups.
- Give each group a piece of paper with one website address written on it and a list of questions underneath. Ask them to look for the answers on the website using the various links.
- Give them 20 minutes to look around the site for the answers. (The websites will have varying amounts of information relating to each question.)
- Get together and go through the answers, discussing what they have learnt.
- Discuss what you should do if you see bullying.
  - What if it was your friend doing the bullying?

Variations/extensions

- Other ideas for adaptation can be be found here:
  http://www.abatoolsforschools.org.uk/resources/key_stage_1_and_2/general.aspx

Cross-curriculum link

- IT

Mix it up

This activity focuses on those being excluded from a group, and the subtle forms of prejudice that this can create.

Suitable for and curriculum fulfilment

- KS2
- Developing good relationships and respecting the differences between people
- To realise the nature and consequences of racism, teasing, bullying and aggressive behaviours, and how to respond to them and ask for help

Aim

- To encourage children to mix with other children outside their normal groups

Resource

- A good understanding of the different groups in the class

Variations/extensions

What to do

- Ask the children to look at one aspect of bullying:
  - Exclusion from a group.
- Ask the children if they think that bullying happens because of lack of understanding of someone else.
  - How can this be changed?
  - Let's have a mixed-up week.
- Get everyone to write down the name of someone they do not normally sit next to at lunch, or who they do not play with in the playground.
  - The teacher will then divide the class into small groups of children who are not normally together.

- This week we must find out as many different things about our new group, e.g. what music they like, what films they like, their hobbies.
  - The more things they find out the more points they will get.
- At the end of the week whoever has the most points gets an extra half-hour of playtime or golden time.
- This can be worked so that everyone can benefit, as each group can reach these goals.

- To produce a Venn diagram showing all the areas where the children have things in common

Cross-curriculum link

- Maths

Stamp it out!

This activity is aimed at understanding that we have to stand up against bullying even if we are not the victim, by making a classroom display of feet to stamp out anti-social and aggressive behaviour.

Suitable for and curriculum fulfilment

- KS2
- Developing good relationships and respecting the differences between people
- To realise the nature and consequences of racism, teasing, bullying and aggressive behaviours, and how to respond to them and ask for help

Aims

- To understand that bullying is anti-social and unacceptable
- To feel united and empowered in standing up collectively against it

Resources

- Whiteboard
- Continuous paper and different paint
- Whose side are you on? CBBC video about bullying:
  www.bbc.co.uk/newsround/13908106
- Quotes from people who have been bullied, have had friends bullied or have seen people being bullied:
  http://news.bbc.co.uk/cbbcnews/hi/newsid_8340000/newsid_
  8346700/8346738.stm
- What constitutes bullying?
  http://www.bullying.co.uk/index.php/young-people/advice/introduction-to-bullying.html
  http://www.bullywatch.org/whatisbullying.html

What to do

- Ask the children if they know what anti-social behaviour (ASB) is.
  - Did they know that it includes bullying and racism?
  - Did they know racism is an act of bullying?
- Outline the definition of ASB and then what constitutes bullying and racism.
- Watch the video and read the quotes.
  - Discuss how they would feel if they were being unfairly picked on.
  - Is that fair or right?
  - How would they feel if it was one of their friends?
- Would they be careful to stay away from the bullies so that they wouldn't be picked on?
  - Is that fair or right?
- So who does bullying affect?
  - Everyone?
- Ask the children if they want to stamp out bullying and racism.
- Get the children to draw around one of their feet.
  - These can be cut out and painted.
- Then ask them to write their name and an affirmative sentence on their foot, e.g. 'There is no place in this school for racism (and sign their name).'
- These can be put up in one of the corridors for all the school to see.

Variations/extensions

- School project to 'Stamp out Bullying and Racism'
- If it is feasible, create an area near or at the gates of the school where footprints can be set into the ground with comments scratched or written on them. This can act as a statement of intent that everyone who enters the school and crosses the footprint threshold is following in the footsteps of past pupils who have taken a stand against bullying and racism

Cross-curriculum links

- Literacy
- Art

Generalisation

This activity is about highlighting and challenging the notion of stereotyping by comparing some examples with the children's own experiences.

Suitable for and curriculum fulfilment

- KS2
- Developing good relationships and respecting the differences between people
- To recognise and challenge stereotypes

Aims

- To recognise and challenge that we cannot generalise about a person without taking that whole person into account
- To understand that everyone is an individual and we cannot make assumptions

Resources

- None needed

What to do

- Ask the children the definition of stereotype.
- Explain to the children that it is a generalised picture of a person created without taking the whole person into account.
- What kind of people do we stereotype?
    - If you wear glasses, does that make you cleverer?
    - If you are overweight, does that make you lazy?
    - If you are a boy, are you better at sport?
    - If you are a girl, are you better at cooking?
- For this activity we are going to look at the concept of categorising, making assumptions and stereotyping.

- Let's write a list together of all the adjectives we can think of to do with stereotypes.
- These should be written on the whiteboard.
- Then ask the children to write about a personal experience when an assumption was made about them according to their gender.
  - You wouldn't be good at football (if you are a girl).
  - You wouldn't be good at cooking (if you are a boy).
- Get a few children to read out their personal experiences.

Variations/extensions

- Find and bring in newspaper clippings that are stereotyping people because of their gender. Ask the children if they can find the articles and identify how they are stereotyping

Cross-curriculum link

- Literacy

What people think of us

This activity turns the tables by looking at what other people think of us and therefore makes us think about how we view other people.

Suitable for and curriculum fulfilment

- KS2
- Developing good relationships and respecting the differences between people
- To recognise and challenge stereotypes

Aim

- To make the class think twice before they make unfair generalisations about people

Resource

These specific stereotypes are about people who live in England
(You will need to do some research on the web if you are teaching in a different country)

- Whiteboard with the following statements:
    - We eat fish and chips every week
    - We have badly made food
    - We are always on time
    - We are always drinking tea
    - We dress in a strange way (socks and sandals)
    - We love pets more than people
    - We eat big breakfasts: eggs, baked beans, toast, sausages and bacon
    - We love gardening
    - Our parks are all clean
    - We like shopping in second-hand shops
    - We have bad teeth
    - We have posh accents
    - We wear bad quality clothes
    - We love football

- We like to play cricket
- We have good table manners
- We have a great sense of humour
- We complain too much
- We talk about the weather all the time
- We have bad weather
- We think we are the centre of the world
- We all love the Queen
- We form orderly queues and get upset at people who cut in
- We are arrogant
- We have 'stiff upper lips' and don't show emotions
- We're obsessed with history
- We have small cars and houses
- We're obsessed with grammar

What to do

- Introduce the idea of stereotyping and its definition.
  (A simplified belief about a particular group, people, country, region or types of individuals.)
- Look at the above statements.
  - Some are true and some are false
- Discuss the different kinds of groups this could be about.
- As you read them out, get the children to put their hands up if the sentence is true of them or in their experience. Mark the total on the board.
- Are these statements correct then?
  - Discuss why it is wrong to stereotype.
  - What would be the best way for these people to see they are wrong?
  - Should we judge people before we get to know them or about them?

Variations/extensions

- Think about how we might stereotype people who live in different countries

Cross-curriculum links

- IT
- Maths
- Literacy

What's my line?

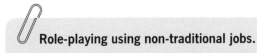

Role-playing using non-traditional jobs.

Suitable for and curriculum fulfilment

- KS2
- Developing good relationships and respecting the differences between people
- To recognise and challenge stereotypes

Aim

- To understand that jobs or extra-curricular school activities shouldn't be based around gender

Resource

- Set of cards with the following jobs written on them:
  - Builder
  - Nurse
  - Doctor
  - Ballet dancer
  - House husband
  - Soldier
  - Nursery teacher
  - Racing driver
  - Hairdresser
  - Model
  - Florist
  - Rubbish collector

What to do

- Explain to the children that you are going to play a game.
- The game is to guess what someone does.
- They are only allowed to ask 10 questions.

- These can be answered yes or no.
- Give the first child a card (if it is a boy try to give him a job not normally associated with boys, e.g. florist).
- The child then performs a short mime of that job.
- The rest of the class ask questions.
- The child can only answer yes or no.
- Then the class have to guess what the mystery job is.
- Ask the children if they presumed that, because someone was a childminder, they must be female. Or because someone was a racing driver they must be male.

Variations/extensions

- Ask the children to quickly draw a portrait of the person doing these jobs; this would be fun as a collage

Cross-curriculum links

- Literacy
- Art

Our class

This exercise only works if there is a diverse mix of children in the class. It is a short discussion-based activity aimed at getting the class to recognise their differences based on how they live their lives outside school.

Suitable for and curriculum fulfilment

- KS2
- Developing good relationships and respecting the differences between people
- To understand that differences and similarities between people arise from a number of factors, including cultural, ethnic, racial and religious diversity, gender and disability

Aim

- To make the class aware of similarities and differences between themselves and other children and that these differences are for many different reasons

Resource

- Whiteboard

What to do

- Talk about how we all live in the same area/town/country, how we all go to the same school and how we all learn and play together, but, when we leave school, do we all do the same things?
- Ask the following questions (choose a few children each time to answer these questions):
  - What do you have for dinner?
  - What time do you have your dinner?
  - What is an important celebration for your family?
  - Does anyone speak another language at home?
  - Do you have relatives in different countries?

- What games do you like playing at home?
- What is your favourite television programme at home?
- What do you listen to at home?
- With each question encourage the child to tell the rest of the class what their answer is and ask leading questions to develop the conversation around the guideline factors.
- Ask about and discuss their answer.

Variations/extensions

- On a world map and choose another culture and explore what they might do at home after school

Cross-curriculum links

- Geography
- Literacy

Worldwide match

This game, suitable for younger KS2 children, is about seeing how we can share many similarities with people all over the world despite other differences.

Suitable for and curriculum fulfilment

- KS2
- Developing good relationships and respecting the differences between people
- To understand that differences and similarities between people arise from a number of factors, including cultural, ethnic, racial and religious diversity, gender and disability

Aim

- To make the class aware that the world is full of people who are similar despite obvious differences

Resources

- Whiteboard
- Game images (see Bespoke resources)
- World map

What to do

- Show the children the characters.
- Ask one child at a time to point out two or more children that have a similarity and explain what it is (it could be racial, religious, gender, cultural (likes), disability or geographical).
- Discuss the fact that we can share similarities with people all over the world even though we may be different in other ways, e.g.
  - Sports
  - Religion.

Variations/extensions

- Choose one or two of the children and look into a day in the life of a child from that country

Cross-curriculum link

- Geography

Bespoke resource

- See worksheet in Bespoke resources chapter at the end of the book

In the know

> The NSPCC have an engaging, very informative magazine called *In the Know* (that can be ordered for free), which is used as the basis for this activity. The activity is about possible serious problems and hardships that face children and how to deal with them.

Suitable for and curriculum fulfilment

- KS2
- Developing good relationships and respecting the differences between people
- To know where individuals, families and groups can get help and support

Aims

- To research and talk about their findings
- To gain confidence through information and knowledge
- To know what to do and where to go

Resources

- Reference:
  http://www.nspcc.org.uk/
- Magazine:
  http://www.nspcc.org.uk/inform/resourcesforteachers/classroomresources/intheknow_wda49558.html
- A list of questions based on information in the magazine to prompt discussion

What to do

- In groups or with individuals, have a list of questions and a copy of the magazine or photocopies of relevant pages from it.
- Ask them to try to find the answers to the questions in the magazine, e.g.
  - What does a social worker do?

- – What is an unhealthy relationship?
- – What types of abuse are there?
- – Why are some children taken away from their families?
- – What should I do if an adult is hurting my friend?
- – Who could I talk to if I have a problem?
- What is ChildLine?
  - – How does a child contact ChildLine?
  - – What happens when a child contacts ChildLine?
- Go through each question with the class and discuss the answers, as well as the broader topic it has highlighted.
- Ask them to do the quiz at the back of the magazine (these can be photocopied).

Variations/extensions

- Base a lesson around the questions at the back asking the children to use the magazine to find out the answers

Cross-curriculum links

- PSHE KS2: 1a,c; 2a,d; 4d
- Literacy

Peace

To teach children the concept of PEACE that comes with finding help and support:

- Practice in asking for help
- Encouragement from meeting others who have overcome challenges like your own
- Acceptance by a group of people who share your feelings and experiences
- Comfort from knowing that you are not alone
- Empowerment through increased knowledge and confidence.

Suitable for and curriculum fulfilment

- KS2
- Developing good relationships and respecting the differences between people
- To know where individuals, families and groups can get help and support

Aim

- For the children to know that they can share their problems and experiences

Resource

- Five A4 cards (blank)

What to do

- Explain to the children that there are many different support groups, where they can get help.
- Teach the children this acronym to help them understand the benefits of using support groups.
- Let's look at what this means:
  - P is for practice to be able to ask for help
  - E is for encouragement that you can succeed too
  - A is for acceptance by a group of people who share your feelings and experiences
  - C is for comfort – you are not alone
  - E is for empowerment – KNOWLEDGE IS POWER.
- Ask the children in small groups of four or five to take a letter.
- Write the letter on one side of the card.
- On the other side draw a picture to represent the meaning.

Cross-curriculum links

- Literacy
- Art

Bespoke
resources

The bespoke resources provided in the following section are those referenced in several of the activities in the book, and are provided in colour and black-and-white for your own use in the classroom, whether used on the whiteboard or as worksheets. We hope that you find them useful.

Chapter 1

Developing confidence and responsibility and making the most of their abilities

KS1

- To recognise what they like and dislike, what is fair and unfair, and what is right and wrong

What I like

Foods I like... mmmmmmmm!
(Draw you favourite food)

I like _____

because _____

_____

_____

It makes me feel...
(Draw how you feel onto this face)

- To know how to set simple goals

It's a goal!

Chapter 2

Preparing to play an active role as citizens

KS1

To be able to take part in a simple debate about topical issues

Pros and cons

Winter A **good** thing about winter is...	**Winter** A **bad** thing about winter is...
Rain A **good** thing about rain is...	**Rain** A **bad** thing about rain is...
Sweets A **good** thing about sweets is...	**Sweets** A **bad** thing about sweets is...
Staying up late A **good** thing about staying up late is...	**Staying up late** A **bad** thing about staying up late is...
Homework A **good** thing about homework is...	**Homework** A **bad** thing about homework is...

- To realise that money comes from different sources and can be used for different purposes

Money!

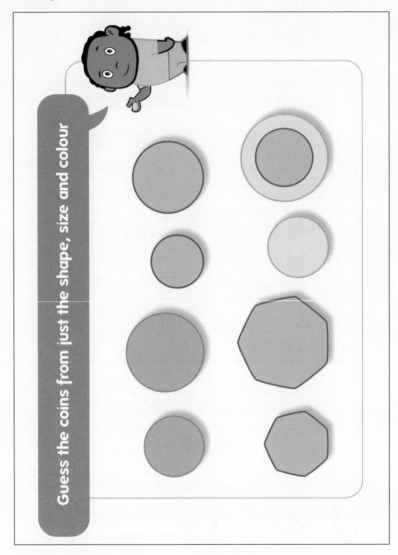

Guess the coins from just the shape, size and colour

*This file to be used on the whiteboard

KS2

- To understand that resources can be allocated in different ways and these economic choices affect individuals, communities and the sustainability of the environment

Finite resources

WATER WE NEED FOR...

We only have ___ units of water available to make food, electricity, to drink and have transport and fun. Think about and choose which columns to fill up and colour them in.

	Food	Transport	Electricity	Tap Water	Fun/Sports
4	TOO MUCH FOOD — we throw a lot away on waste dumps because we can't eat it all	TOO MUCH TRANSPORT — we all have our own cars, boats and helicopters	TOO MUCH ELECTRICITY — we have all the heating, lighting we want, watch tv all day, leave everything on	TOO MUCH TAP WATER — we have all the water we need, we can waste as much as we want	TOO MUCH FUN/SPORTS — we all have swimming pools, water lights every night in our own fountains
3	LOTS OF FOOD — we all have lots of vegetables as well as meat	LOTS OF TRANSPORT — we have trams, buses, boats, lots of aeroplanes and we all have cars	LOTS OF ELECTRICITY — we have lighting, hot food, tv and computers when we want it them	LOTS OF TAP WATER — we have enough to drink and a bath every day	LOTS OF FUN/SPORTS — local swimming pools and water parks, grass on sports patches
2	JUST ENOUGH FOOD — everyone gets just enough food but it's only vegetables	JUST ENOUGH TRANSPORT — we have buses, trams and boats, a few aeroplanes but no cars	JUST ENOUGH ELECTRICITY — we have lighting, hot food, tv and computers 3 hours a day	JUST ENOUGH TAP WATER — we have enough to drink and only enough for 1 bath a week	JUST ENOUGH FUN/SPORTS — local swimming pools, grass on sports pitches, no water parks
1	NOT ENOUGH FOOD FOR EVERYONE — enough for the rich but not enough for the poor	SOME TRANSPORT — we have bicycles, boats and trams but there are no cars or aeroplanes	SOME ELECTRICITY — we have lighting, hot food, 1 hour of tv and 30 mins of computer time a week	SOME TAP WATER — we can use the taps for 1 hour a day	SOME FUN/SPORTS — a swimming pool in every city, no grass on sports pitches or in parks
	NO FOOD — we all starve	NO TRANSPORT — we all have to walk everywhere	NO ELECTRICITY — we have no tv or heating, we sit around candles at night eating cold, raw food	NO TAP WATER — we all die of thirst	NO FUN/SPORTS — no swimming pools or water parks, no grass in parks or on sports pitches

- To explore how the media present information

Scoop!

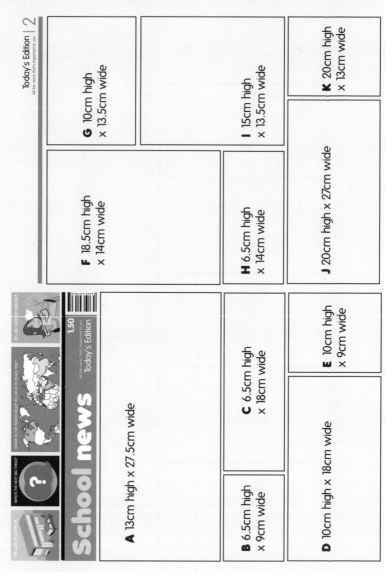

Today's Edition | 2
All the news that's important to you

G 10cm high × 13.5cm wide

I 15cm high × 13.5cm wide

K 20cm high × 13cm wide

F 18.5cm high × 14cm wide

H 6.5cm high × 14cm wide

J 20cm high × 27cm wide

school news
Today's Edition
All the news that's important to you
1.50

WHAT'S THE NEXT BIG THING?

WHERE IN THE WORLD MIGHT YOU BE IN 20 YEARS TIME?

DO I OR I MAYBE FIND ISH?

BE AMAZED WITH THIS

A 13cm high × 27.5cm wide

C 6.5cm high × 18cm wide

B 6.5cm high × 9cm wide

E 10cm high × 9cm wide

D 10cm high × 18cm wide

Chapter 3

Developing a healthy, safer lifestyle

KS1

- To understand how to make simple choices that improve their health and well-being

My healthy meal

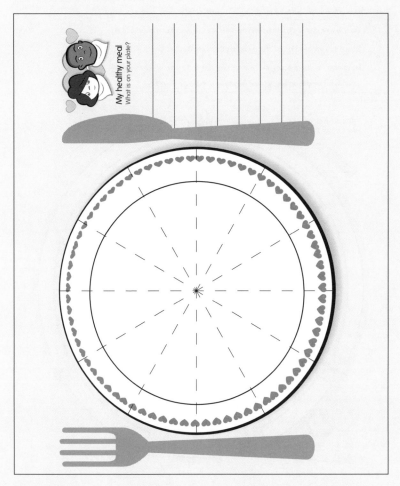

KS2

- To understand what makes a healthy lifestyle, including the benefits of exercise and healthy eating, what affects mental health and how to make informed choices

Recipe for life

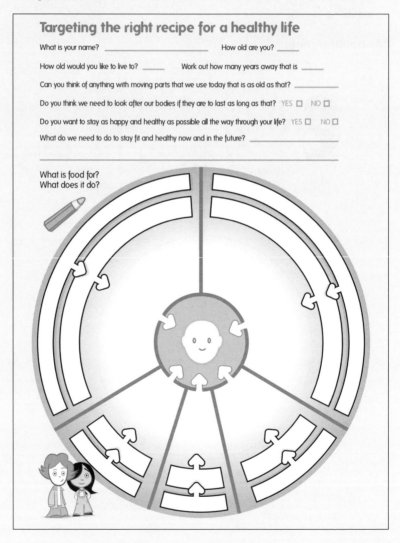

Targeting the right recipe for a healthy life

What is your name? _____   How old are you? _____

How old would you like to live to? _____   Work out how many years away that is _____

Can you think of anything with moving parts that we use today that is as old as that? _____

Do you think we need to look after our bodies if they are to last as long as that? YES ☐   NO ☐

Do you want to stay as happy and healthy as possible all the way through your life? YES ☐   NO ☐

What do we need to do to stay fit and healthy now and in the future? _____

What is food for?
What does it do?

- To be able to recognise the different risks in different situations and then decide how to behave responsibly, including sensible road use, and judging what kind of physical contact is acceptable or unacceptable

Action groups

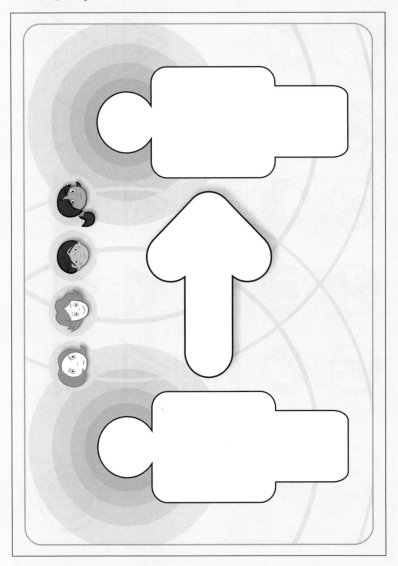

- To know the school rules about health and safety, basic emergency aid procedures and where to get help

Read the signs

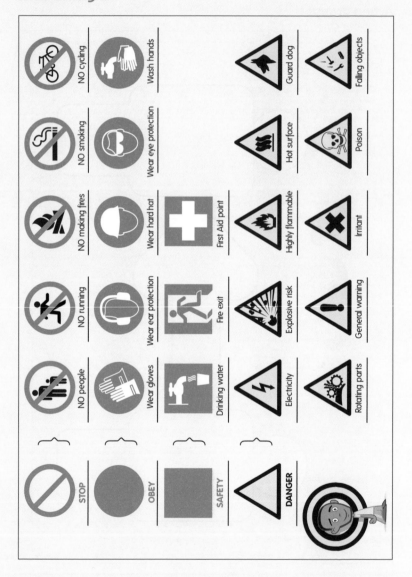

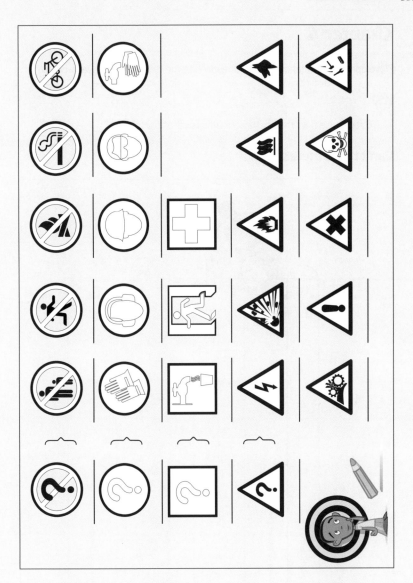

Chapter 4

Developing good relationships and respecting the differences between people

KS1

- To recognise how their behaviour affects other people

Can't be bothered

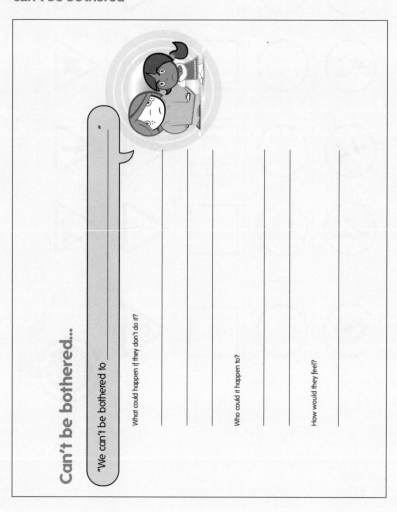

Can't be bothered...

"We can't be bothered to _____

What could happen if they don't do it? _____

Who could it happen to? _____

How would they feel? _____

KS2

- To be aware of different types of relationship, including marriage and those between friends and families, and to develop the skills to be effective in relationships

The 3 Rs of a relationship

The 3 Rs of a relationship	Parent/Guardian	Best friends	Other children	Teacher
Roles Different things you should do for each other. *e.g. Friends* *- treat each other as equals* *- stand up for each other*				
Rules How to treat each other. *e.g. Friends* *- be kind* *- help each other* *- be thoughtful*				
Rituals Things to do regularly together. *e.g. Friends* *- spend time together* *- always say hello and goodbye*				

- To understand that differences and similarities between people arise from a number of factors, including cultural, ethnic, racial and religious diversity, gender and disability

Worldwide match

Differences and Similarities
Children around the world

Jenny
Great Britain

Afro Caribbean
female
likes reading & playing guitar
Christian

Denna
Israel

Arabic
female
likes drawing & horse riding
hard of hearing
Jewish

Aalim
Saudi Arabia

Arabic
male
likes reading & cars
Muslim

James
Australia

Chinese
male
likes barbecues & trains
Buddhist

Lara
Brazil

mixed race
female
likes football & barbecues
Christian

Nyla
Pakistan

Asian
female
likes drawing & playing guitar
vegetarian
Muslim

Bryn
South Africa

Asian
male
likes cricket & playing piano
Hindu

Ania
Canada

Asian
female
likes horse riding & playing
computer games
Hindu

Mai
China

Chinese
female
likes basketball & computer
games
wears glasses
Buddhist

Yousef
Morocco

mixed race
male
likes football & playing piano
Muslim

Jordan
Jamaica

Afro Caribbean
male
likes cricket & basketball
hard of hearing
Rastafari

Robert
Great Britain

white
male
likes trains & football
vegetarian
wears glasses
no religion

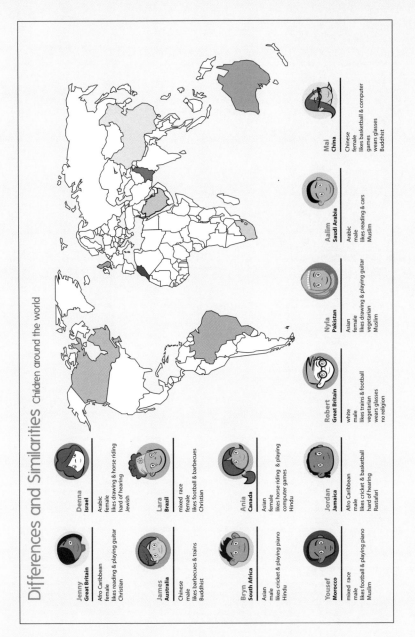

Differences and Similarities Children around the world

Jenny
Great Britain

Afro Caribbean
female
likes reading & playing guitar
Christian

Denna
Israel

Arabic
female
likes drawing & horse riding
hard of hearing
Jewish

James
Australia

Chinese
male
likes barbecues & trains
Buddhist

Lara
Brazil

mixed race
female
likes football & barbecues
Christian

Bryn
South Africa

Asian
male
likes cricket & playing piano
Hindu

Ania
Canada

Asian
female
likes horse riding & playing
computer games
Hindu

Yousef
Morocco

mixed race
male
likes football & playing piano
Muslim

Jordan
Jamaica

Afro Caribbean
male
likes cricket & basketball
hard of hearing
Rastafari

Robert
Great Britain

white
male
likes trains & football
vegetarian
wears glasses
no religion

Nyla
Pakistan

Asian
female
likes drawing & playing guitar
vegetarian
Muslim

Aalim
Saudi Arabia

Arabic
male
likes reading & cars
Muslim

Mai
China

Chinese
female
likes basketball & computer
games
wears glasses
Buddhist

*This file to be used on the whiteboard